Their Search
for God

WAYS OF WORSHIP
IN THE ORIENT

by
Florence Mary Fitch

Illustrated with Photographs
Selected by
Edith Bozyan, Beatrice Creighton
and the Author

★

LOTHROP, LEE & SHEPARD, NEW YORK, N. Y.

ACKNOWLEDGEMENTS

The author gratefully acknowledges her indebtedness to the many authors and sources whose studies furnish the background for this work, and to the friends, both in the East and the West, who have given insight and suggestions. It is impossible to mention all who have made contribution to this book, but the following have read the manuscript in whole or in part or have given other special assistance:

Pearl Buck, President of The East and West Association; Mahatma Mohandas Gandhi; Shiva Prasad Gupta, Benares, India; Dr. Ananda K. Coomaraswamy, Curator of the Oriental Department of the Boston Museum of Fine Arts; Mrs. Donna Luisa Coomaraswamy, author; Swami Nikhilananda, Ramakrishna-Vivekananda Center, New York; Ramkrishna Modak, Clergyman and President of the One World Association, and Mrs. Manorama Modak, author, Ahmednagar, India; Mrs. Jessie Heinrich, United Presbyterian Mission in the Punjab, India; Dr. Shao-Hwa Tan, Minister Plenipotentiary, Chinese Embassy in Washington, and Mrs. Mary Huang Tan; Dr. Yi-Pao Mei, Professor Yen Ching University, Peiping; the late Dr. George D. Wilder, Professor Yen Ching University and Peiping Union Bible School; Dr. Lewis Hodous, Former President of Foochow Theological Seminary, China, Emeritus Head of Chinese Department, Hartford Seminary Foundation; Dr. Wynn C. Fairfield, General Secretary, Foreign Missions Conference of North America, President of the Associated Boards for Christian Colleges in China; Miss Kazuko Higuchi, Assistant in Art, Wheaton College; Dr. Alexander Soper, Associate Professor of History of Art, Bryn Mawr College; Dr. C. Burnell Olds, missionary in Japan, founder of the Interfaith Club in Okayama; Bhikku Dhammapala, Udawath Temple, Kandy, Ceylon; Mrs. Vivienne Vitharana, Kandy, Ceylon; Rev. Gyomay M. Kubose, Buddhist Church of Chicago, Illinois; Dr. Walter M. Horton, Professor of Theology, Oberlin Graduate School of Theology; Dr. Clarence H. Hamilton, Former Professor of Philosophy, Nanking University, China, Professor of Philosophy of Religion, Oberlin Graduate School of Theology; Eleanor Newcomb, Wellesley, Massachusetts; Ann Harbourt, Cleveland, Ohio.

Thanks are also due to the many museums and photographers who have furnished the illustrations, and to the India Office of the Standard Vacuum Oil Company, who cooperated so cordially and whose photographers took many pictures especially for this book.

CONTENTS

FOREWORD

Every person lives in two worlds—the outer one which he can see and hear and the inner one which he can feel, the world of his hopes and fears, his thoughts, his loves. His efforts to relate the two are part of his religion.

Ideas about the inner world and about God, the Supreme Being, are different in different countries. So are the forms of worship in which they express themselves. It is difficult to appreciate those which are unfamiliar; the deepest significance of any religion is found by those who have grown up in it and lived it. Yet whoever studies a religion other than his own with an open mind will find his horizon widened and will discover new values. The universal truths of religion ought to draw people together. "The broadminded see the kernel of truth in all faiths, the narrowminded see only the differences."

This book seeks to present what is most distinctive and valued in Hinduism in India, Confucianism and Taoism in China, Shinto in Japan, and then Buddhism, which, beginning in India, has spread eastward through Asia and beyond. It does not include Islam, the religion of the followers of Mohammed, even though it is the second largest religious community in India and a powerful force in all Asia. Islam had its origin in the Near East as a daughter religion of Judaism; its beliefs and practices were influenced by Jewish and Christian thought, in connection with which it should be studied.

"Bow down and worship where others kneel, for where so many have
been paying the tribute of adoration, the kind Lord must manifest Himself."
—RAMAKRISHNA.

Their Search for God

Ways of Worship

in the Orient

*"Many millions search for God
and find Him in their hearts."*

In India, the temple is the center of life.

THE HINDU WAY

IN INDIA, religion has a more important place in life than in any other country in the world. One reason may be that the people have less of other things to give color and purpose to living. Two-thirds of the Indians are so poor that they have scarcely enough for food, clothing, and shelter, and nothing at all for even the simplest pleasures. But there are other reasons why the religious spirit has permeated the whole life of the Indian people. To the Indian there is no separation between the outer world of things and the inner world of the spirit. The body is only a cloak which covers and almost conceals the spirit which is the real part of man. What is true of man is true of everything. There are spirits everywhere. Everything is part of the Infinite Spirit. All life is one; all life is sacred. This is the kernel of Hinduism.

Gandhi, the outstanding leader in India's struggle for independence, is a Hindu. He lives with austere simplicity and devotes several hours before dawn to study and meditation. He is the helper and friend of even the humblest people. He believes that evil can be conquered, not by anger and violence, but by non-violent resistance and patience. He has taught his followers to trust in soul-force. He has prayed and fasted as penance for his own or his country's mistakes. He has chosen to endure imprisonment rather than sacrifice his convictions. The people call him "Mahatma," Great Soul.

There are numerous religious groups in India—Moslems, Sikhs, Christians, and others—but most of the people are Hindus. Their religion, so old that no one knows when it began, is Hinduism. Hindus believe that God is everywhere, that everything is part of the Universal Divine Spirit. The goal of each man's life should be to know this Universal Spirit, which Hindus call Brahman.

It is not easy to understand this Brahman who is present in the deepest part of every soul. Many centuries ago a boy asked his father to explain it to him. His father told him to put some salt in water and bring it to him the next day. When the boy brought it, the father said: "Where is the salt?" The boy could not see it. Then his father told him to taste

11

For every Hindu child, the goal of life is to know Brahman, or God.

the water; all of it was salty. "So, my son," the father said, "you do not see Brahman, but it is in all; it is within your own body."

Hinduism teaches that there are three paths by any one of which a person may become free from the narrowness of his own small self and become conscious of his oneness with Brahman, the Divine Self. So it should be possible for every one to find his way to God.

The most difficult path is that of spiritual insight, the path of the mystic. The Hindu who follows this path gradually ceases to think of himself as all-important, or even as a separate individual. He comes to identify himself more and more with Brahman, in whom he and all other life have their being. This selflessness is not learned easily, but comes from long hours of meditation and concentration. "All is Brahman—my self within my heart, smaller than a grain of rice; my Self within my heart, greater than the earth, greater than the heaven."

The second path is that of works; it requires faithfulness to daily duties and to the ritual of worship. This path leads to God only when all deeds are performed in quietness of spirit, without desire for personal gain or power, when one forgets self in serving God. The devout Hindu goes to his day's work, conscious that to work is to worship, for he is filling the place God has assigned to him, and if he is not faithful, his land and his people cannot prosper. His work is his religion, his duty.

Then there is the path of loving devotion to God. So plowmen in Bengal sing:

> "Till my heart, O Beloved, as I till this land
> And make me thine as I make this land my own."

The goal of all three paths is the same. Thousands of Hindus repeat daily the ancient prayer—"As different streams, having different sources, all find their way to the sea, so, O Lord, the different paths which men take all lead to Thee."

ALL LIFE IS SACRED

The Hindu believes that Brahman expresses some part of his life in every living thing, and so to kill even the smallest insect is wrong.

The cow is sacred in India and wanders freely wherever it will.

Animals deserve gentleness and care and should not be treated as though they exist only for the use of men. "He who cannot make alive, may not slay" is the rule.

A person who has become one with the Universal Spirit finds "the life-breaths of other creatures as dear to him as his own." He "does naught to others which, if done to himself, would cause pain." Hindus are taught "ahimsa," harmlessness, to inflict no injury whether for personal pleasure or gain or out of hatred and passion.

In early days the chief wealth of India was cattle. Cattle drew the plow, carried burdens, and provided food and drink. Since Indians never forget a favor, one of their oldest laws states that the cow is holy and is not to be killed even for sacrifice. So the cow is one of the family, like the cat or dog in western homes.

Cows wander freely about the country and even along city streets. In the early morning they stop at open doors where hospitable and devout women are ready to hand out freshly baked cakes or some greens. They call expectantly at vegetable stalls and are not disappointed. They are not driven off from any grassy spot they may find, even though it is difficult to grow grass in dry sections of this hot country. In times of drought, the famished cows are driven to streams and springs where people share with them their scanty water. No traffic policeman ever brings cars to a standstill more suddenly than does a cow who chooses to cross a crowded city street.

The cow is a symbol of motherhood and many of the simple people still believe that worship of her is one way to insure the birth of sons.

THE HINDU DEITIES

The westerner is overwhelmed by the many gods of Hinduism and the mass of details in the representation of them. Ignorant people in India think of them as the gods who preside over different clans or localities or who protect from different misfortunes. The intelligent Hindu regards them all as attempts to express various aspects or activities of the Infinite, who is so great that no image can be like Him, no words can describe Him. Whatever is said about Him is only part of the truth. It is not even correct to call the Infinite "Him", for that seems to say that He is Father and not Mother, whereas He is both.

Shiva, Lord of the Dance, who at the close of each cycle of the world's history, dances it out of existence and dances in a new cycle. The flaming arch surrounding him is the universe; the demon under his feet is matter, destroyed in the onward rush of the Divine Spirit. This is the spiral dance of the whirlwind, symbol of the elemental divine force which in nature ever destroys and ever makes new.

The three most important deities are Brahma, Vishnu, and Shiva. They are the Hindu trinity. Sometimes they are represented by one figure with three heads and six arms but only one body, to show that they are not really three distinct persons but one person with three activities. Brahma is the Creator of all; Vishnu is the Preserver, who keeps the world going; Shiva is the Destroyer, who brings the old to an end that the new may be born. Vishnu, the Preserver, has come to earth from time to time and lived among men. He is worshiped most often through his two incarnations, Rama and Krishna.

Another popular deity is Ganesa, who has an elephant's head. His mother, wife of Shiva, was mother of all the world, but she longed for one baby all her own, so she made a doll and nursed it as a real child. Vishnu was sorry for her and he entered into the doll and gave it life. Then one day a spirit with the evil eye looked at the beautiful child and its head dropped off. The mother was heartbroken, but Shiva promised that he would get another head for the boy, the first one he could find. Just then one of his warriors came in with a splendid elephant head, which Shiva put upon the child. The Mother grieved because her son was now so ugly that no one would want to worship him. To comfort her, Shiva decreed that, for all time, whoever worships Ganesa at the beginning of any undertaking shall have success.

There are thousands of deities in India, enough for every person to have his own. Each family chooses one from among these many manifestations of Brahman as the special object of its devotion. The family sanctuary is dedicated to him; his image or symbol stands upon the altar. According to Indian belief, God is everything; he may be worshiped in any object—a stream, a bit of bright cloth—but an idol is the most usual form. The idol is not God nor even a likeness of him, for no one knows how God looks; but it may suggest his character. It may have many faces because God sees and knows all, many hands because he can do many things.

For a festival in honor of a particular god, a family makes a clay image and invites the spirit of the god to enter it for the celebration. When the ceremony is over, the spirit leaves and the image, having served its purpose as a temporary residence, is thrown into a river or temple tank to make certain that nothing defiles it.

The Nandi, a sculptured bull, kneels in adoration at Shiva's temple, for the bull is Shiva's steed.

Krishna is often represented playing his flute. The flute is a symbol of the call of God to man.

Ganesa, the god of success, removes all obstacles, guards households, and, being the scribe of the gods, helps book-keepers, authors and school boys.

Maidens searching for Krishna. According to legend, all maidens were drawn to Krishna as the individual soul is ever drawn toward the Universal Soul.

Shrines are everywhere in India, wherever people pass. Under a lonely tree, whose very existence in the hot city street makes it seem divine, there may be the symbol or image of some god. Here children on their way to school and men on their way to work drop flowers or pour a bit of refreshing water. Before a few rough stones marked with red clay a peasant leaves his gift to propitiate the goddess of some dread disease, to insure success in some new undertaking, or simply to express gratitude and devotion. It may be a single flower, a bit of red string, a fragment torn from a garment, or a tiny saucer of oil with wick freshly lighted. One who is too poor to have even these may name over the gifts he would like to make and the god will accept his thought.

Every village has one or more temples. Within a courtyard is a tank for ceremonial bathing and the shrine where the patron god is worshiped. At least once a day a priest performs the ritual to insure the deity's protecting care for the village, and people who wish may watch and share in the ceremonies. The congregational worship of the West is not found in Hinduism; most worship is individual.

Some large cities, like the cathedral cities of Europe, have enormous temples which rise above all the homes, dream castles of strength and unreality. They have many courts, long dim corridors, and vast halls. Fantastic figures of animals and gods, such as no man ever saw, are carved into the walls and twined around the pillars; they suggest the fullness of life of the All-pervading Spirit, which not even the most fanciful art exhausts. Here is a world of life and richness set apart from the drabness and poverty outside its walls.

Such a temple is almost a village in itself. Priests, attendants, and servants live there. There are shops where objects for sacrifice are for sale, courts where the temple cows and elephants are kept, gardens to provide flowers and leaves for the altars, a tank where the devout may bathe before worshiping, and open cloisters where people gather to hear the priest recite the scriptures. There is merit in listening even if one does not understand. Only men of the higher castes may enter the innermost sanctuary of the patron god, but others may bring gifts to the lesser deities. No one appears empty-handed. The offering may be a coconut broken at the feet of some image or melted butter that is poured into a little lamp at the altar with a prayer: "May my life be like a lamp, its flame carrying my spirit toward God."

At the Madura temple, the largest in India, Shiva and his wife make an occasional tour of the temple by night, each riding on a gold-covered horse. They are accompanied by other gods, elephants, musicians, and chanting priests, and followed by the crowd. As the procession makes its solemn round, there is no light but that of torches and the hundreds of little lamps which outline the doorways of the vast dim halls and the arches of the colonnades.

HOME WORSHIP

Schools and offices open late in India so that the morning worship may be unhurried. Even so the Hindu household is astir long before daylight. A man may spend two or three hours at his morning devotions. To prepare his mind and heart for prayer, breathing exercises are most important, as breath is life, the most real thing about the body. He breathes out and in, then for a moment stops breathing; he breathes first through one nostril, then the other, and with each breath repeats to himself the word "Om," the shortest form in which one can name the Infinite Spirit. Next he tells his rosary, a chain of one hundred and eight seeds or beads, fingering each seed with a prayer. Now it is time for worship in the family sanctuary, the most holy place in a Hindu home. Every family that can afford it has a private priest and a separate room, often on the roof.

The women rise earlier than the men, and even the children are wakened with the first streak of dawn, for "no one may greet the sun from his bed." In the freshness of the morning, both body and mind are made clean for the day. The old rule holds for all, "No eating without praying; no praying without bathing."

Each woman takes her part in the religious ritual of the home. The oldest woman prepares the family shrine, placing before the symbol or image of the god the "five-fold offering" of flowers, fruit, water, light, and incense. The other women may join her and the children, one or two at a time, go with her carrying their offerings. As soon as the sun rises, some go out to salute it, for the ancients taught that the rosy dawn is the daughter of God himself.

In the center of the women's court in a white-washed pot upon a white pedestal, stands the sacred tulsi tree. Each morning one of the

RIGHT: *Fantastic figures of animals and gods, carved in the wall and pillars, all have religious significance.*

BELOW: *The temple at Madura, the largest in India. The devout bathe in the tank before worshiping and people gather in the cloisters to hear the priests recite the scriptures.*

women makes the first offering of the day by pouring holy water upon the earth and over the tree. She makes the lucky mark upon the trunk with fragrant sandalwood ash. Then the others follow her as she walks around the tree five times, repeating sacred verses.

The Hindu kitchen is almost as sacred as the shrine, for all food is part of the Divine Nature and must be touched and eaten with reverence. The woman who is to do the cooking pays special heed to the ritual of bathing and puts on fresh clothes before entering the kitchen. Unless servants are of as high a caste as the family they serve, they are not allowed even to clean the kitchen floor. If even the shadow of a person of a lower caste falls upon food, it is unfit to eat and will be thrown out. The offering to fire is given twice a day, morning and evening, before eating; for Agni, the god of fire, has done the cooking and surely he should be fed first. Fire from the family hearth is placed on the altar. Water is poured around it and an offering is made with the prayer:

> "May all in the world be happy;
> May they be healthy;
> May the rain come down in the proper time;
> May the earth yield plenty of food."

It is now six or seven o'clock. Early tea or fruit may be served but there are two more ceremonies before breakfast. Servings of the food are taken out for a holy beggar who may be at the door. Grain is thrown out for crows and crumbs for insects. This is the gift of hospitality. Then food for the gods is carried into the sanctuary by the woman who has prepared it and the family priest performs the morning worship in the presence of the men. These gifts for the needs of others, whether insects or gods, train the Hindu to share with others as a matter of course and help him to remember that all life is one from the very lowest to the highest.

Breakfast comes last in the morning program. Each wife serves her husband as if he were a god, and it is part of her worship that she fast until after he has eaten. At midday again there is private prayer and meditation.

The twilight hour, "the hour of union between darkness and light," the hour when man's soul most easily finds itself one with the Infinite Soul, is called in India "the cowdust hour." It is then that the cows return to their homes, and blessed is he who "takes the dust of their

Making a pattern of powdered rice on the threshold is part of the early morning ritual. This is worship of the spirits that guard the entrance of the home.

feet" with reverence. Women go to the roof-tops for meditation. Bells in home and temple call men to evening worship. The ancient prayer is repeated:

> "O God, lead me from darkness to light,
> from the unreal to the real,
> from death to immortality."

THE CASTE SYSTEM

In India class is determined for life by one's birth. There are four main classes, called castes. Each has a particular part to play in the life of the country. Hindu children do not have the problem of deciding what they will do when they grow up; boys will carry on the work of their fathers and girls will marry boys of their own caste. They are trained in accordance with the duties of their caste, their "dharma." One of the most sacred texts is "Better one's own duty, though imperfect, than the duty of another well discharged."

As Hindus believe that religion is the most important business of life, the most honored caste is that of the priests, called Brahmins. It has been their responsibility for many centuries to perform the religious ceremonies, to preserve the Indian sacred scriptures, and to teach. Most of the Brahmins earn their livelihood in other ways, usually in the professions, but they should always observe the careful ritual of prayer three times a day and give part of their time to religious teaching and counsel and conduct worship for those of other castes.

The second caste, called Kschatriya, is that of the warriors and rulers. It is their duty to protect the weak and helpless, to relieve suffering, to punish wrong-doers. Like the knights of mediaeval Europe, they are trained to control themselves that they may be able to control others with justice. They should never hate, never fear; though strong, they should be humble and gentle.

The third caste, that without which all others would be impossible, is that of the Vaisyas, the farmers and traders. It is their obligation to do their work in the spirit of service rather than for selfish gain. These three castes are called "the twice-born." Below them are the Sudras, the fourth caste, which includes artisans, laborers, and servants. There are many subdivisions of each caste.

The cow-dust hour, when cows return to their homes. Blessed is he who "takes the dust of their feet" with reverence.

—A RAJPUT PAINTING OF THE 18TH CENTURY.

People of various castes may be friendly neighbors and may have business dealings, but the strict Hindu will not eat with anyone who is not a member of his caste, never with a foreigner, and he will not allow the marriage of his child to one outside his caste. The honor of his birth must be guarded for his children's children. A Brahmin may cook for a Sudra, but a Sudra is not allowed to cook for a twice-born Hindu. A household with servants must have many. The one who cooks will not clean the kitchen, the one who brings in the water will not carry out the refuse.

There are hundreds of thousands in India who are outside any caste. Some of these have made themselves outcastes by disregarding the caste rules; others are descendants of the tribes living in the land before the Aryan ancestors of the present Indians came in from the north; in that respect they are like the Indians of North America. They live on the edge of every town and do the work which no caste person is willing to do.

The caste-system has given stability to India's social life and security to the individual. Every boy knows what his work will be and that the members of his own caste will stand by him in any emergency.

Today industrialization and city life are breaking down many barriers, but caste-distinctions persist. A Brahmin may choose among many occupations, but he will not disregard caste rules. A Sudra, or even an untouchable outcaste, may secure education and wealth and enter one of the many new vocations; yet he does not rise out of his caste, but he raises his caste by his influence. A rich Sudra may provide education for a promising boy in order to have a suitable husband for his young daughter.

Caste is forgotten when any man relinquishes the worldly life and becomes a holy beggar, giving up home and possessions and devoting himself entirely to God and the life of the spirit. He may have been of any caste and is received by any, for "in Brahman, there are no distinctions." "The wise see the same in all—whether it be a Brahmin, endowed with learning and humility, or a cow or an elephant or a dog or an outcaste."

Brahmins have no monopoly of religion. "Though not a Brahmin, you may live like one," is the high ideal which many a father and mother hold before a child. The foremost religious leaders through all the centuries have not come from the professional Brahmin class, and they do not today. Gandhi is a Vaisya, of the merchant caste.

This baby of the "untouchables" may be some day one of the leading men of India.

HINDU CYCLE OF LIFE

The Hindu cycle of life has four stages, each with its obligations. In the first period, childhood and youth, the boy learns both practical work and the things of the spirit. The second period begins with marriage; the youth, now a householder, has children of his own and works for the support of his family. So far the Hindu thinks of life as do people in any other country. But his religion has taught that, as soon as his eldest son can carry on, a man has fulfilled his obligation to his ancestors, and, especially if he is a Brahmin, he should retire from the life of a householder and give his devotion to the gods.

In this third period of life, men used to live in the forests as hermits. Even today there are some such, and sometimes a grandfather in the home lives almost as a hermit, giving his time to study and meditation.

The last stage of life, never attained by more than a small proportion of the people, is that of the "sannyasi," a traveling teacher. Eight months of the year the sannyasi travels, stopping along the way in family courtyards. He repeats long passages from the sacred writings, sings the old folk songs, and recites prayers. He tells stories to the children and sometimes does tricks of magic. During the growing season he rests in some temple court or in a hillside cave, lest he trample down the new life springing up in all the country-side. The presence of a sannyasi near a village is a blessing. The children carry food their mother has prepared, leaving it near his cave or sheltering tree, and then, a little over-awed, run for home. The men gather in the evening to hear what he has learned in his wanderings. A father may ask him to remain in his home as the "guru," spiritual teacher, of his young son.

Some sannyasis are also "yogis," which means that they have attained union with Brahman, the Supreme Soul. Often disciples spend months or years with a yogi that, through discipline of breathing, posture, meditation, and concentration, they may learn his spiritual insight and his control of body and mind. The holy men of India, free from all worldly motives and so free from all evil, are considered the chief glory of Hinduism. To serve them is a privilege. The people gladly support their sannyasis, as mediaeval rulers in Europe supported their artists, and modern Americans endow research laboratories.

From the forest-dwellers have come the greatest religious teachings of India. The forest-dweller was a holy hermit. Boys came to him for training and older men to talk over their problems. For the Indians, woods and hills, birds and beasts, empty spaces and the wide-spreading sky are a call to meditate, a way to God.

—RAJPUT PAINTING OF THE 19TH CENTURY.

HINDU SCRIPTURES

Some of the Hindu scriptures are so sacred that they may not be read by any except the twice-born, and may not be repeated within the hearing of any woman, Sudra, or child. These are the "revealed" writings. They consist of three groups — the Vedas, the most ancient verses of prayer, the Brahmanas, rules laid down by the Brahmins for the worship ritual, and the Upanishads, the answers of the forest-dwellers to questions about God, man, and the universe. There is also much "remembered" traditional literature, which anyone may hear. The most familiar and honored of these remembered scriptures are two epics. One of these gives the story of Rama.

Vishnu, the great Protector, seeing the evil done by Ravana, the lord of demons, came to earth to destroy him. He took the form of a young prince, Rama. For some time he lived in the forest, where he and his younger brother Lakshman were trained by a hermit. He became strong in body and skilled in all the crafts of woodsmen. When he returned to his father's home, he won a contest to draw a divine bow and received as his bride the princess, Sita. When a younger wife of Rama's father demanded that her son Bharata be made heir to the throne, Rama gave up all his rights and made a vow that he would go into exile in the forest for fourteen years. Sita and Lakshman went with him. Soon after, the father died of grief and Bharata, more loyal than his mother, sought his brother Rama, and urged him to return to the kingdom. Rama replied that he must fulfil his vow for the fourteen years. So Rama, Sita and Lakshman lived as hermits, made friends of the wild creatures of the forest, and fought to protect the helpless.

One day when Sita was alone, a beggar appeared and she gave him food. Immediately, the beggar, Ravana in disguise, seized her and carried her off in his waiting chariot to Ceylon. Her husband and brother searched for her nearly a year. Finally, Hanuman, son of the Wind God, who was able to fly far above the earth, discovered her whereabouts. He was general of all the monkeys, and he summoned his forces. Across the water that separates Ceylon from India they made a bridge of their own bodies, bound together by their tails. They fought and destroyed the demon-armies. Rama, who followed them, killed Ravana with his

Rama gave Sita a necklace of pearls and precious gems, but she took it from her neck and placed it around the neck of Hanuman, the most clever, valiant, and devoted servant of man.

—RAJPUT PAINTING ABOUT 1600 A. D.

celestial sword. He rescued Sita and ·vent back to the forest. When the fourteen years of his vow were over, Rama and Sita returned to his kingdom, which he ruled with justice for many years.

The second epic tells of the bitter rivalry between two families of cousins, the Kurus and the Pandus. Both sides appealed to Krishna for divine help. He gave each the choice between one hundred million warriors and his own presence. The leader of the Kurus chose the many warriors to swell his already powerful ranks, but Arjuna, leader of the Pandus, chose the Divine Companion, who became his Charioteer.

As the opposing armies stood face to face, Arjuna's heart failed him. He cried out, "These are my kinsmen; I cannot kill them."

Then Krishna told Arjuna to shake off his faint-heartedness and stand up like a conqueror. "Neither for the living nor for the dead do the wise grieve. The body may be slain, but not the Self that dwells in the body; that Self is not born, nor does it die when the body dies.

"Remember your own dharma. To a warrior nothing is better than a righteous war. If you are slain, it is an unsought door to heaven; if you are victorious, you will enjoy this world. To say, 'I will not fight,' is to think of yourself more than of your duty. Do your work as a warrior, but do it for the welfare of the world, not for any gain for yourself."

Arjuna advanced into battle and won a glorious victory. So the kingdom was restored to the eldest brother of the Pandus. His reign was long and noble and prosperous. After the custom of India, when he grew old, he, his wife, and his brothers retired to the Himalayas where they hoped to find the celestial region. The queen and the four younger brothers died on the way. The aged king remained, his only companion his faithful dog.

He was walking on sadly, when the chariot of the mighty storm-god Indra descended beside him and Indra invited the king to ascend to heaven. He hesitated, thinking of his wife and brothers. Indra assured him that they were already in heaven. Then the king said, "My faithful dog must go with me." Indra protested that there was no place in heaven for dogs, but the king replied, "I shall not cast off my dog. I shall never give up a person that is devoted to me nor one that seeks my help till my own life is gone. This is my vow."

Then Indra praised the king, saying, "You have mercy for all creatures. You have renounced the chariot of heaven instead of renouncing your dog. There is no one in heaven that is equal to you." The king was taken up to heaven and reunited with his wife and brothers.

*The palaces and temples of the warrior caste suggest the setting for
many of the heroic tales of India's past.*

RITUALS OF CHILDHOOD

When a baby is born in India the children and women announce the glad news, blowing a conch shell as they go from courtyard to courtyard. Every one is doubly happy if the baby is a boy, for only a son can carry on the family name and only a son can save his father's soul from misery after death. "There is no heavenly region for a sonless man."

On the name-giving day, the baby is brought for the first time out of the tiny room in which he was born into the principal room of the house to begin his life as an individual. A name is chosen very carefully. The first letter should be taken from the stars under which the child was born. It is well if the name contains the name of some god, for then, whenever the parents call the child, they acquire the merit which comes from the mention of a god's name.

There may be a special ceremony when the child is given rice, his first solid food, and another for the first ceremonial cutting of the hair. The priest cuts the hair, leaving a sacred top-knot, which every twice-born Hindu should wear.

The most significant occasion in a boy's life, if he belongs to one of the three higher castes, is when he is invested with the sacred cord. It comes between the age of seven and twelve, earlier for the Brahmin than for the Vaisya, and marks his initiation into his father's caste. This is his second birth, the beginning of his higher, more spiritual life. Thus he becomes one of "the twice-born." In a Brahmin home at least, the boy will have had careful preparation from the family guru.

The family puts up a booth in the courtyard for the worship of Ganesa, the fifteen Mother Goddesses, and the sacrificial fire. The boy's head is shaved, except for the top-knot. He and his guru seat themselves near the fire. The boy holds in his hands the sacred cord and slips it over his head as his teacher prays for strength, long life, and illumination for him. He whispers to the boy a new name, used only at this ceremony, a name known only to himself, his guru, and his God. This symbolizes his individual, unique relation to the Infinite Spirit. Then the guru reminds the boy of the duties of his caste and he promises to fulfil them. A silk shawl is spread over the heads of the two and the guru whispers into the boy's right ear the sacred text: "Upon the

Young mother, standing in magic square made of various kinds of grains, is asking the sun god, Surya, to protect her child.

excellent glory of the Creator may we meditate; may He Himself direct our thoughts," words so sacred that they make the ear holy for life, words which he will repeat every day as the first prayer of the morning.

After this ceremony is over, the boy, even though only seven years old, has become a man. He will live in the men's quarters and eat with them. If a Brahmin, he is expected to worship three times daily as his father does and study the sacred writings; thus he will carry on the splendid tradition of study, self-control, and the pursuit of spiritual understanding.

No matter what caste a girl is born into, her dharma is to be a good wife and mother. The first prayer of every Hindu girl is "Make me a good wife; give me a good husband and may he live long and may we have many sons." She is trained to be efficient, self-controlled, unselfish, gracious, and, if possible, beautiful. She learns the ritual of the bath and of dressing. She must know the foods which strict Hindus may eat, excluding meat, eggs, and certain vegetables and grains, and how to cook according to ritual rules as well as to make food wholesome and attractive. She must understand the duties and honor of her caste and the various practices of religion expected of women, including the self-discipline of many fasts.

In some parts of India, a special month is set aside for small girls to worship the family cow. They make the sacred red mark on the cow's forehead and offer it bananas rolled in fine, sacred grass. The girls pray first for the cow, then for their little world and themselves.

> "May disease be far from you, Mother Cow.
> Cow Mother of the world, be always full of milk.
> By caring for you, may we live in comfort.
> And may there be blessing to me."

At other times she sits beside the cow before milking; she feeds it, strokes it, and calls it pet names, and the cow gives milk freely as she would to her own calf, for, the Hindus say, "Milk is the only food that is the product of love." And the little girl gains "a lucky hand with cows," which is important for a wife.

In the spring comes the chief festival that is especially for young girls. The forms vary in different sections of the country, but the purpose is the same, to pray for a good husband, many sons, and death before her husband's.

Girls gather for their spring festival before dawn on five successive mornings. They go together to the river where they mark an enclosure with rice paste; within it they build a small altar and seats for the ideal wives of Hindu tradition whom they invite to join them. They worship them and pray that they too may have good husbands and many sons.

MARRIAGE

"There are no unmarried women in India." The exceptions to this statement are very few, for the Hindu scriptures state that there is no heaven where the parents of an unmarried girl may go.

Marriage is usually arranged by a go-between who knows the families. The traditional custom is that the boy and girl do not meet, but the parents may visit each other's homes and see the possible son- or daughter-in-law. When they are satisfied, an astrologer studies the horoscopes of the young people to see whether they agree; if so, the engagement is announced at a Blessing Ceremony. Later the astrologer selects the wedding day; it must be in a lucky month, and the sun and moon and Jupiter must be favorable.

Each day during the last week, the family priest reads to the bride about her duties as a wife. He reads in Sanskrit, the ancient, sacred language, which she does not understand, but she does understand that marriage is a very solemn event with which the gods are much concerned.

In a Brahmin home the marriage is most often at the "cow-dust hour." The bride and groom are each veiled, since neither may see the other until the ceremony is over. They are led separately into the marriage booth in the courtyard where the sacred fire is burning. The bride's father and mother worship before the fire and then they both give the bride away. The priest ties bride and groom together with a silken scarf and repeats words of blessing. Standing beside the fire, they pour butter onto the flames, as the priest repeats marriage texts. The most solemn and irrevocable act is the rite of the seven steps around the sacred fire. With each step the groom makes a promise to his bride and at the seventh says, "Take this step with me and become my friend and follow me." After the priest sprinkles the couple again with holy water, they thank the gods for the happy wedding and dismiss them.

In some districts, the bride's mother brings food on a single plate and for the only time in their lives, husband and wife eat together. This is a sacramental meal, uniting their lives so that they are no longer two persons but one. No husband or wife will thank the other; for does the head thank the hand?

"Not for the love of the husband, is the husband dear,
But for the love of the Soul, is the husband dear.
Not for the love of the wife, is the wife dear,
But for the love of the Soul, is the wife dear."

—FROM THE UPANISHADS.

Marriage in India is a matter of serious family concern. The girl accepts a new responsibility as a member of another family, whose welfare she is expected to put before her own. She hopes to like them, but it is her dharma to attain perfection as wife and mother even if she does not. She relinquishes all thought of herself as distinct from her husband. And a good husband responds with love and tenderness. "Where women are honored, there the gods are pleased; where they are dishonored, religious acts are of no avail." Husband and wife should know that the love they share comes from that larger Soul which includes them both and all life. In such selflessness, love is made deeper and the individual self finds himself not lost but richer.

The Hindu believes that what stirs a man's heart most deeply and joyously is an experience which his god shares and that through his personal love he may deepen his consciousness of unity with the Divine. This belief gives rise to the idea that every god has a wife or wives and that the whole universe is feminine to Brahman, the Divine Lover.

A woman's haunting fears are two—lest she have no son, in which case her husband may bring home another wife, no matter how tenderly he still loves her, and lest she may be left a widow with no hope except that she may die soon and perhaps in the next life be her husband's wife again. To this day it is true in general that the only unmarried women in India are widows.

DEATH AND REBIRTH

When a man is about to die, his friends make offerings to help him across the dark river which flows between the earth and the abode of Yama, who rules over the dead.

The Hindus burn their dead before sun-down. Every community has its burning-ground, near a stream if there is one. The sons lay the logs and place the body upon the pyre and the eldest lights the fire. The spirit rises in the flames, free from the worn-out body, which is an offering to Agni, god of fire. When the fire has burned out, the chief mourner gathers the ashes and throws them into the river.

On the tenth day after death comes the most important rite in Hinduism, Sraddha, the ceremony that assures the departed soul safe passage to the court of Yama and merciful judgment there. It also gives

Widows in India wear white saris without borders. Today there are
schools which train them to be teachers, nurses, and nuns. Now it is
not unusual for widows to remarry.

the dead man the body he needs until he is again born on earth. This rite is effective only if performed by a son.

Although rebirth is not mentioned in the "revealed" scriptures, most Hindus believe that one lifetime is too short to attain perfect union with God. To get rid of pride and anger and selfish desires and all that is mean and small is a slow and difficult process. God gives each soul a series of second chances until perfection is attained.

A person seldom carries with him any memory of his former life, but he does carry the results of the life he lived; what he wanted, what he thought, and what he did determine whether his new birth will be more or less fortunate than the one before. If he was greedy, he may be reborn a pig; if he was lazy, he may be a tree that never moves; if a man of low caste was faithful in his worship, he may be reborn a Brahmin; if a man has been unkind to his wife, he may become a woman; if a woman has all the virtues of a good wife and mother, she may be re-born a man. The thought of rebirth is a great motive to fidelity to one's dharma or duty. Whatever a man's luck, it is not chance nor fate but the result of his own past.

This idea of transmigration, so distinctive of Hinduism, is due perhaps in part to the tropical climate. Instead of sharp contrasts of seasons, with much life ending with oncoming winter and new life bursting forth in the spring, life and death exist side by side in boundless profusion and the one passes into the other in an endless cycle.

KARMA

"Karma" is the name the Hindus give to the accumulation of desires and thoughts and actions which a person carries with him from birth through death to birth again in an endless chain. When a baby dies, they say, "Its karma must have been very bad." An old man has certainly brought good karma from his earlier lives, and, if he has lived well, will carry still better into the next life.

In every living thing a portion of the Divine is struggling ever upward. No one should injure needlessly even a worm. The humblest creature may, after several rebirths, become an honored member of one's own family. All life is one; all life is sacred.

Along with the newer scientific knowledge, Hindu boys are still taught the doctrine of Karma—that whatever life brings is a result of their own past.

HINDU FESTIVALS

The Hindu New Year, like the Jewish, comes in the fall. Hindus believe that this day determines the character of the whole year, so every one is up early to make a good start. As with every festival, there are extra bathing and praying, new clothes to wear, elaborate meals, and special cakes. At night houses are decorated with lights. This is a time to make up quarrels; those who call ask forgiveness if they have wronged anyone during the year.

On the second day of the year, Yama, the Lord of Death, takes a vacation to accept the invitation of his sister to a feast. So every brother should visit his sister and share with his brother-in-law the feast the sister has prepared. Later in the year there is a return festival in which the brothers invite the sisters back to the family home as most honored guests.

In February or March a gay festival called Holi recalls the legend of a witch who was burned. A great pile of fuel is heaped up to represent the witch. On the first day of the festival children go from house to house as American children do on Hallowe'en, beating drums and singing and asking for food and fuel for the fire. The evening of the second day the fire is lighted. All march around it singing songs to show their hatred of the witch as the symbol of evil. In many courtyards the old witch is ignored, and Holi is the "Swinging Festival." The children in their gay clothes stand on boards hung from the flowering trees to see who can swing highest; even the grandmother, who in India may be very young, joins in the sport.

In August comes the celebration of the birthday of Krishna, most beloved of all the gods. The evening before people gather in the temple to hear the story of his birth. At midnight the doors of the inner shrine are opened for every one to see the baby Krishna in his cradle. The crowd greets him with shouts and throws grain and money upon his shrine. The priest bathes the little image in the five nectars—milk, curds, melted butter, honey, and sugar. The next morning further ceremonies are held in the temple; then the image is carried to the river and thrown into the middle of the stream so that nothing may defile it.

Women and children on their way to a temple festival.

In most homes, Sarasvati, goddess of wisdom and art, is honored in the early fall. Every one lays before her the tools of his occupation; the artist's brush, the musician's instrument, the carpenter's square, the farmer's hoe, the women's pans, the children's books are included in the worship, for all have power to bless and serve.

The autumn festival of the Divine Mother, the wife of Shiva, is one of the most universal. For days before, minstrels wander through the streets singing her praises. In every household, the father and children make an image of her, standing upon a lion with a spear in her hand, about to destroy a demon, the symbol of evil; often she is given ten heads and ten hands to indicate her many activities.

On the opening day of the festival, the priest sprinkles the floor and all objects of worship with water made holy by invoking the presence of the seven holy rivers of India; then he invokes life into the image by prescribed words and movements. After the Great Mother has entered the image, the priest offers her the universal gifts of love—flowers, incense, light, food, and water. He chants hymns in her honor and prays: "May this worship be accepted by Thee, O Mother! Whatever defects there may be of word or ritual or devotion, graciously forgive all."

The last three days of the year are the festival of Diwali, the Feast of Lights. All over India at the cowdust hour small spears of flame appear, outlining windows, balconies, doors, and garden walks. Hundreds of little lamps are made in every village every year, but each girl works with greatest care on her own particular lamp, putting her mark upon it. At the end of the day, if the town is near a river, she will set her special light on a tiny raft and watch it drift away; if the light burns until it reaches the other shore or has drifted out of sight, there will be good luck until the next Diwali.

On the second day ghosts are on the street, so wise people stay at home, amusing themselves with stories of those who have been brave enough to encounter the ghosts. Hanuman, the monkey-god, who is the guardian against evil spirits, is honored at this time.

On the last day, account books are worshiped, for Diwali is the festival of Lakshmi, the goddess of wealth. The priest blesses the books and the house saying, "May you be happy all the year." The new book is left open all night and is blessed again in the morning prayer.

At the close of the autumn festival of the Divine Mother Goddess, which is universally celebrated, boatmen row her image down the river where they will lower it into the water.

PILGRIMAGES

Every orthodox Hindu wants to make a pilgrimage before he dies to at least one of the sacred places of his holy land.

Benares on the Ganges is the most sacred. Every Hindu child has heard the story of the birth of this wide, deep river, which Shiva let fall from the coils of his hair. He gave its waters power to heal all diseases and wash away all evil, and to give new life to any one whose ashes it touches. Pilgrims bathe in its waters and fill jars to carry home to purify the household shrines and to heal the distant sick. The aged pray to die beside the river that Mother Ganga may receive their ashes and that their spirits may pass at once to heaven. The children of Benares play upon the broad steps and peddlers cry their wares; cows, goats, dogs wander at will; crows keep up incessant chatter. At the water's edge the people bathe, the family laundering is done, brass pans and kettles are scoured. Amidst all this turmoil, on little turrets or platforms, on tiny rafts along shore, men worship, absorbed in meditation, undisturbed by all that goes on around them; for to the Hindu all life is sacred, all life is one, all forms of life are expressions of the one Universal Spirit.

In the crowds at Benares there are many sannyasis with begging bowls, the holy men who are now living out the last stage in the Hindu cycle of life. The true sannyasi honestly seeks to free himself from himself. He would not think of anything as his own, not even his body or his thoughts. He does not want to be a separate individual, for he knows that the self apart from God is nothing. When he took the sannyasi vows, a priest performed the Sraddha funeral ceremony for him, indicating that he had already died as a separate self; from then on, his only life has been loving and knowing God. When physical death comes, he will not be born again on earth, nor go to some heaven for temporary happiness. His spirit will not persist as a distinct person, but will return to God, the Infinite Being from which all life comes. As the ocean draws its water from many streams, as the honey in the comb has been gathered from many flowers, so, the Hindu scriptures teach, will human lives end in God and final peace.

Benares on the Ganges. Every day, pilgrims crowd the flights of steps that lead down to the sacred river. According to Hindu belief, the waters have power to heal all diseases and wash away all evil.

THE WAY OF CONFUCIUS

THE NAME "CONFUCIUS" is the westerners' attempt to write the Chinese K'ung-fu-tzu. This means Honorable Teacher K'ung, for the Chinese write the family name first. Some eighty generations of K'ungs, including the recent premier of China, have been his descendants. Confucius thought of himself as "not a creator of ideas, but a transmitter, believing in and loving the ancients," whose words had been handed down through countless generations.

YANG AND YIN

The early Chinese religion was based upon the idea that all things have come into being through the interaction of two forces, Yang and Yin. They are the spiritual and material elements of the universe, which never exist apart from each other. The most familiar Chinese symbol, a circle bisected by an S curve, represents them. Yang is the male, Yin the female. Yang is light, Yin darkness. The sun and fire belong to Yang, the moon and water to Yin. When Yang is in the ascendancy, there are warmth and life, but if his power is unchecked, drought and fever may result. When Yin is in control, cold and death, floods and chills follow. For an ordered life, Yang and Yin must work harmoniously in rhythmic alternation. Heaven is the Yang principle, earth the Yin. Heaven and earth complete each other. Man, nourished by the earth, strengthened and sustained by Heaven, supplements them both. Religion is not apart from life but it runs through all life; it is the give and take between human life and Heaven and earth.

THE WAY OF THE ANCIENTS

Since the most important factors of life for the early Chinese were the family and the land, their religion took two forms—worship of ancestors and worship of gods of the soil.

In a home where old traditions are followed there is a shrine or shrine room where tablets bearing the names of the family dead are kept in a cabinet, or, if the family is very poor, written on a paper which is pasted on the wall. When the father dies, a tablet is inscribed with his name and placed in the shrine, and that of his great, great grandfather is removed and put in a storage room. The tablet of the founder of the family remains permanently in the cabinet.

Every day the mother places flowers and food on an altar in front of the tablets and the father burns remembrance incense. He lights three sticks of incense, holds them in both hands high above his head, and places them in a burner. Each member of the family kneels three times and each time bows his head to the ground three times. The "three kneelings and nine knockings" are a kow tow and express reverence and gratitude; in many modern families a bow replaces the kow tow.

To the Chinese, the world of the living and the world of the dead are one. They honor their ancestors with special feasts on anniversaries of their births and deaths; they remember them in all family festivities, inform them of any important events in the family life, and consult them in times of crisis and anxiety. They believe that their ancestors have more power and wisdom than when they were living, and are able to share these with their loyal and humble descendants.

The Chinese bury their dead in mounds on the family land, where the spirits always remain. The family graves must never be neglected. It is not often that an eldest son will leave the old home, but if business makes it necessary, his family will remain behind that they may care for the graves and worship before the tablets, and that the children may grow up under the influence of their ancestors.

When the head of the family dies, the sons may divide the property and establish their own homes. In this way many a family has grown into a clan and the large family court has become a village. There often is a memorial temple for the clan, to which relatives who live in other villages return for special festivals. Representatives of the various branches of the family serve as a council to distribute any joint income and to consider common problems. If anyone is in trouble, help is given; if the clan is prosperous, education is made possible for those who are ambitious and promising. Honor to one is honor to all, disgrace to one is disgrace to all, including the ancestors.

In China, the larger the family the happier the grandfather. The ideal is "five generations in one courtyard."

Seldom does a junk set out to sea without burning incense at its little shrine to the goddess of the sea. All along the coast of China are temples where local magistrates perform worship to her "that the sea may be calm and the waters pure."

An abundant rice crop is insured and floods prevented by making sacrifices to the river spirits.

In ancient times the worship of the gods of the soil was one of the chief concerns of organized society. The first place of worship was a mound of earth, a symbol of these gods. Offerings made here insured a good harvest. Later square altars were built, for the early Chinese people pictured the earth as square, bounded on each side by one of the four seas. The altars were open to heaven that its rain and sunshine might make the earth fruitful. Families built their homes around the common altar and so villages began; the altar court was the center of all social and civic life. The head man of the village officiated at the sacrifices; there were no professional priests. Each district and province had its altar, but the most elaborate and impressive was the Altar of Earth in the northern suburb of Peking. This was the capital city and the emperor made the offering in behalf of the entire country at the summer solstice. Every village still has its shrine to the local god.

Mountains and rivers were also worshiped by the ancient Chinese. Four mountains, one for each of the four directions, were regarded as sacred because mountains have power over wind and rain. Later the Chinese chose a central mountain and four on the outlying frontiers and worshiped them, too. These nine sacred mountains are visited by pilgrims from all over the country. Sacrifices are made to the river spirits for the benefits they confer, for the terrors in time of flood. To guard against the perils of the sea the Chinese make offerings at shrines along the coast and on every outbound boat.

Heaven is exalted above all other nature-gods. It controls the movements of sun and moon and stars; it regulates the seasons and brings the succession of night and day; it is Shang-ti, the Ruler above. The emperor was "the Son of Heaven," a humble little child. He united Heaven and earth, as the peasant united earth and man.

For centuries before the end of the empire in 1911, the Chinese emperor conducted the worship of Heaven at the winter solstice. With the passing of this shortest day of the year, the sun was beginning its triumphal march from the south; Yang, the principle of Heaven, was once more in control.

Now China has no emperor and no state worship; no procession fills the terraces of the Altar of Heaven with its music and incense and rituals. But its broad base rests securely on the good earth; its gleaming marble receives the sunshine and rain which Heaven sends; it is an enduring reminder of that three-fold harmony of Heaven and earth and man upon which all well-being depends.

The white marble Altar of Heaven stands in a large park in the southern suburb of Peking. Only eighteen feet high, it has a series of three terraces, each one approached by steps on the four points of the compass. From the center of the upper terrace, nothing is visible but the overarching sky. Here is no irreverent towering toward Heaven, but humble clinging to the lowly earth; no temple wall to shut men in, but open readiness to receive the benedictions of the Supreme Spirit above.

THE TEACHER OF ALL CHINA

Chinese civilization is said to have had the longest continuous development of any the world has known; even when conquerors overran the country, they did not destroy the culture but themselves became Chinese. This stability is largely the result of the teachings of two men, Confucius and Lao-tzu, who lived in the sixth century before Christ, and of firmly established customs, "ancient" even in their times.

At the age of twenty-two Confucius gathered a group of young men around him and began to teach. His way of teaching was to talk with them of government, of literature, and of life. He accepted any one who came to him, but he was impatient with lazy students who would not think for themselves. "Rotten wood cannot be carved," was his comment. "When once you learn a thing, you must never give up until you have mastered it. If another man succeeds by one effort, you will use a hundred efforts. If another man succeeds by ten efforts, you will use a thousand efforts." This has been quoted often in the desperate years of China's history.

He never forced his will or opinions upon his pupils; he wanted to teach them how to learn more than what to learn. He used simple, concrete, every day examples to teach his doctrines. He believed that a man must approach every problem, person, or thing from within, not from without, putting himself into each experience.

Confucius had the humility of true greatness. His disciples reported that he would not allow the use of "shall," "must," "certainly," and "I." He was in love with the literature of his people and never was satisfied or weary in his study. The Chinese Classics include material which Confucius collected and selected, many of his own sayings and incidents about him recorded by his disciples, and writings of his followers. Among them are historical notes, practical directions for government and for personal and social life, a book of odes, and a book of rites. Confucius advised his young grandson to begin his education with the study of the odes because poetry, art, and music create a sense of oneness with all men and all natural objects. This oneness is the source of all wisdom and right living.

Confucius loved music and ceremonies. He thought they helped men

The Classics have been the text-books in Chinese education and the maxims of Confucius are taught in every home.

to order their lives and their human relationships according to Tao (pronounced Dow) which is the way and will of Heaven. True culture combines outward form and inner genuineness, beauty and sincerity. "When the solid outweighs the ornamental, we have boorishness; when the ornamental outweighs the solid, we have superficial smartness. Only from the proper blending of the two will the higher type of man emerge."

"Li" (pronounced lee), meaning propriety, Confucius thought of as the central principle unifying all his teachings. It includes ceremony and courtesy, but is more than these. It is being sensitive to any situation and responding in the suitable way. It rests upon a fine sense of personal dignity and respect for nature and for all beings.

Reverence toward parents and consideration for others are the foundation of goodness, for it is in the family that a child first learns fellow-feeling and cooperation. All right behavior depends upon such oneness with other people, "jen" (pronounced run) the Chinese call it. "Keep the balance true between yourself and your neighbor," taking yourself as the basis for treating others. "The man who has 'jen,' wishing to establish himself, will have others established; wishing to succeed, will have others succeed." One of Confucius' disciples asked, "Is there one word which may serve as a rule for all one's life?" and the teacher replied, "Is not reciprocity such a word? What you do not want done to yourself, do not do to others."

The Classics list five relationships in life where jen and li must be applied—those between ruler and subject, between father and son, between husband and wife, between older brother and younger brother, between friend and friend. In China today, even among the humblest people, an appeal to li will bring a quarrel to quick settlement. The one who is in the right remembers the principle of jen and does not press his advantage but allows his opponent to "save his face," that is his self-respect.

Confucius spoke often of the "princely man" in contrast with the "little man," who has never outgrown childishness. Man is by nature good and if he develops normally he realizes his own being with dignity and grace and meets with fidelity his obligations as a member of society. The princely man is not such by birth or class, but by his own discipline.

Reverence for parents is "the fountain whence all other virtues spring."

There are many princely men in China today. They may live in poverty but they walk with dignity. They respect themselves; they belong to a family and they will not be soon forgotten; they have a share in ancestral lands; they enjoy the simple pleasures of their food and drink, the warmth of sun, the moist earth after a spring rain, the gatherings of neighbors, the village festivities, and the old, old wisdom of the Classics, read or handed down by word of mouth.

Confucius held public offices for many years. Finally he gave up public life, but not his concern for good government. He thought that a ruler should be an example for his subjects, as "the north star keeps its place and all stars turn toward it;" his right to rule depended upon his ability to maintain the well-being of the people, whom Heaven loves. If anything went wrong, if there was drought or pestilence, he must do penance. If he failed in his duties, his people had the right to revolt, for Heaven speaks in the wisdom of statesmen and in the power of revolution as well as through the emperor.

Some one asked, "What are the requisites of good government?" Confucius replied, "Food, military equipment, and confidence of the people in their ruler." Asked which of these should be given up first, he said, "Military equipment, and next food. From of old, death has been the lot of men; but if the people have no faith in their rulers, there is no standing for the state."

He believed that the best ruler governs but little; he seeks to develop the character and culture of his people. Government begins with the individual's control of himself and advances with the self-discipline of the family, the village, the state, and the nation; it will end only with the harmonizing, "even-ing up," of the world, which will bring not world empire, but world peace.

Confucius had little interest in the religious observances of his time and taught little about religion apart from everyday life. His religion was faith in Tao, the way of Heaven. He wanted to make every part of life, inner purpose as well as outward ceremony, conform to Heaven's way. He said: "The power of spiritual forces in the Universe—how active it is everywhere! There is no place in the highest heavens above or in the deepest waters below where the moral law does not reign."

Confucius died at the age of seventy-three and was buried in a grove where he had often taught. With the passing of the centuries, the honor accorded Confucius increased until he who had been first a teacher of a few private pupils became the "Teacher of all China."

"The Grave of the Most Holy One" is approached through a long avenue
of cedar trees in an enclosure where any descendant bearing the name
K'ung is allowed burial.

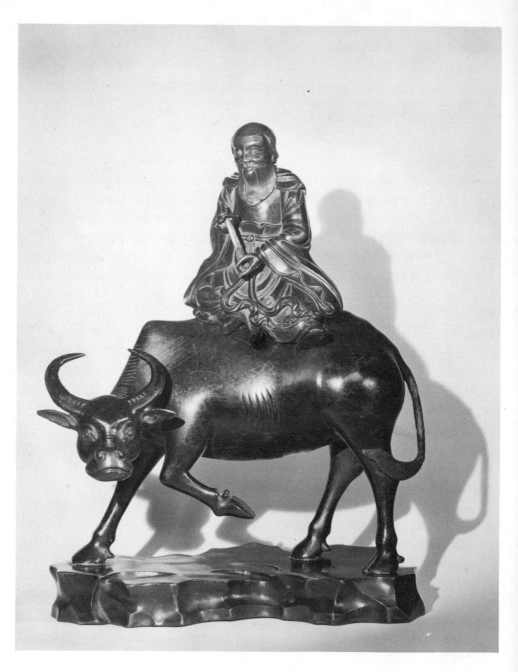

According to tradition, Lao-tzu left his home, riding on his water buffalo, to carry his teachings to the West.

THE WAY OF LAO-TZU

WHEN CONFUCIUS WAS STILL A YOUNG MAN, tradition tells us, he went to see Lao-tzu, the most distinguished scholar in his province, keeper of the library in the capital city. As he spoke to him of his efforts to improve the disordered conditions of his time, Lao-tzu said: "Mosquitoes will keep a man awake all night. In the same way this talk of duty to one's neighbor drives me nearly crazy. Keep the world to its original simplicity. As the wind bloweth where it will, let virtue establish itself." When Confucius returned, one of his disciples asked him what teaching he had given Lao-tzu. He replied with awe, "I saw a dragon in the heavens. How could I teach him?"

Like Confucius, Lao-tzu was distressed by the disorder of his time but he thought it a mistake to try to regulate man into goodness. Man is by nature good. Trust his unspoiled instincts; he does not need external control, if only he is responsive to Tao, the Divine Way. Excessive regulation of life hampers the development of the individual.

Lao-tzu found the simple, untroubled life impossible in his home-city. He started out to find a haven in the remote west. Tradition records that, when he reached the border of the state, the official refused to let him pass until he should put down his teachings in writing, which he did. These words have been preserved in a little book, compiled and edited later, known as Tao Te Ching, the Scripture of the Divine Way to Virtue. Nothing was heard of him again; but China—both west and east —has remembered his word that the law of life is Tao; to trust life and adjust to it, to relax rather than to struggle, to live simply, freely, this is to be wise and good and contented. Man and nature and Heaven are one whole. A man's spirit is liberated when he is willing to be himself, not struggling for what is beyond his own powers, content to share the freedom of the One Spirit which is in all.

To explain Tao, Lao-tzu used words that recall the Hindu insistence that Brahman cannot be defined or described, "The Tao that we talk about is not the Tao in itself. No name that we give it will abide forever."

"When we look at it, we cannot see it;
    When we listen to it, we cannot hear it;
    But when we use it, it is inexhaustible."

This is an immediate, mystical experience. When a man is responsive to the Divine Nature and does not seek to force his own will or cherish his own opinion or press his own advantage, his eyes become open, his understanding grows. Thus Lao-tzu taught twenty-five centuries ago what modern scientists have learned, that they must humbly learn nature's ways and work according to her laws, if they would have her serve them; man is free only when obedient.

Lao-tzu taught "inaction." He did not mean that man should do nothing, but rather, that he should not make life artificial, he should be natural and spontaneous. "Who can make muddy water clear?" he asked, and added, "But if allowed to remain still, it will gradually become clear of itself. Nothing in the world is more soft and weak than water; yet, for attacking things that are firm and strong, nothing surpasses it."

Lao-tzu was an old man when he wrote his book and he must have been lonely, for he said, "My words are very easy to understand, very easy to practice: but the world cannot understand them nor practice them."

"The fewer persons know me,
    The nobler are they that follow me.
    Therefore the Sage wears coarse clothes,
    But he keeps a jade in his bosom."
"I have three treasures which I hold fast and prize.
    The first is gentleness, the second frugality,
            the third humility.
    Be gentle and you can be bold;
    Be frugal and you can be liberal;
    Avoid putting yourself before others
    And you can become a leader among men."

To "recompense injury with kindness" was a natural consequence of this teaching. "To the good I would be good; to those not good I would also be good that I may make them good." Confucius was once asked what he thought of Lao-tzu's principle of returning good for evil. He replied, "What then is to be the return for good? Rather should you return justice for injustice, and good for good."

68

"Keep the world to its own original simplicity. The heron is white without a daily bath. The raven is black without coloring itself."—LAO-TZU

Lao-tzu believed that the political order would operate as noiselessly as does the natural order if those in authority had no selfish ambition, if they did not meddle nor exact too heavy taxes. "The empire is a divine trust and may not be ruled. He who rules, ruins; he who holds by force, loses." Lao-tzu would have "war horses become plow horses" and each community live in isolation and peace. He would have people return to simple ways, "find their plain food sweet, their rough garments fine, and be content with their homes." "When your work is done, retire into the background; for this is the way of Heaven."

"The cause of Heaven's and earth's eternal duration
Is that they do not live for themselves,
Therefore they can perpetually give life.

So the Chosen One places his self hindmost and it comes foremost.
He renounces his self and his self remains preserved.
Just because he does not care for his own,
Does that which is his own become perfected."

One of Lao-tzu's most illustrious followers told of an old man with no garment but a skin bound around his waist, walking along a road singing. One who met him asked him why he was so happy, and was told: "There are many reasons. Of all created beings, man is highest and I was born a man. Of man, there are male and female, and I was born a male. Of those born, many never outgrow swaddling clothes, but I have reached ninety years. Poverty is the common lot of all; death is the goal of all. I have shared the common lot and now draw near the goal. Why should I not be happy?"

Although Confucius and Lao-tzu disagreed as to how the ideal society was to be brought about, both urged their followers to consider the ways of the world they knew rather than to concern themselves with mysterious spirits. Both tried to get rid of superstitious forms of worship. Lao-tzu thought that it was impertinent to try to force Heaven by magic and insisted that spirits could do no harm to the man who followed Tao. But neither teacher gave the people a substitute for the spirits they believed in. Ordinary people, anxious and in trouble, want some divine help close at hand; they will worship anything rather than nothing. So all the old superstitions and magical practices continued among the masses.

The Eight Immortals, celebrated in Chinese literature and art, were thought to have their home on islands in the eastern sea, where grew an ambrosial plant with the elixir of life and where the inhabitants were immortal.

Some seven hundred years after Lao-tzu, a religious sect was organized which adopted him as its patron and his book, Tao-Te-Ching, as its scripture. It called itself Taoism and is counted one of the chief religions of China. Lao-tzu himself would not be very proud of his connection with it, for it emphasizes all that he and Confucius tried to banish from religion. Its followers believe that, since Tao is greater than nature, they can develop supernatural powers; they use many devices to foretell the future and to work magic. Their chief interest has been to secure immortality. They searched for fabled islands in the eastern sea where grew an ambrosial plant with the elixir of life and where the inhabitants were immortal. The Taoists concocted pills of eternity which should give power over death. In doing this they learned much about herbs and, all unconsciously, were pioneers in the science of botany. Of course, even those who took the pills died in due time, but they believed that in the spirit world they would enjoy unending, happy lives similar to those they had lived on earth.

Some Taoists tried to win harmony with Tao in ways similar to those of the Indian mystics. They became hermits, living in mountain caves and forests, practicing "inaction" very literally. A few such hermits still live in remote places, but popular Taoism today is a religion of the ignorant, who accept its superstitious beliefs without question because they seem to give help in the present life and hope for the life to come.

SOCIAL AND RELIGIOUS CUSTOMS

Every one in China lives consciously or unconsciously under the influence of both Lao-tzu and Confucius. Confucian ethics regulate almost every relationship of life. Although modern studies have an important place in Chinese education today, the Classics are still honored both in school and in the home. The grandmother orders all the affairs of the household according to the family book of ceremonial law. The Book of Great Learning has said: "The tranquility of the world depends on rightly governed states. A rightly governed state necessitates well-regulated families. A well-regulated family is made possible only by the self-culture of the individuals composing it." Children are told stories from the Book of Filial Piety, which recount the sufferings which ideal sons have endured to serve their needy parents.

The story-teller in the market place repeats the fairy tales and stirring legends of China's past.

Respect for learning is universal in China. No greater honor can come to a family than to have one of its members win recognition as a scholar.

In China, learning begins early.

Taoism, with its belief in spirit-powers and its persistent faith that life is good, brings in the mystical and gay and playful. When parents know that a child is coming, they have special ceremonies to keep evil spirits away. Later they send announcements of the birth, written on red paper, for red is the color of Yang and brings good luck. Gifts pour in; a month later, eggs dyed red are sent as a return gift, an odd number for a boy, even for a girl, for odd and even are Yang and Yin. The child's name is chosen by the father, usually after consulting an astrologer, and is then approved by the head of the family. Often the real name is not given at first; little children are called by number, "first boy," "second sister," and so on. The boy, of whom the family is so proud, may be called by the name of a girl or of an animal, or an even worse name, so the spirits will think he is of no account and not steal him. Thank offerings are made when the baby is a year old and again on every birthday, until he is sixteen.

Some parents take the baby to the temple and buy a charm. It may be of gold or of scraps of paper upon which the priests have written words that are believed to have power to protect the child from illness and misfortune. If the child is taken sick, a priest is called to recite sacred texts, for such words have power to heal.

In China a youth is not considered an adult until he is married. As elsewhere in the Orient, marriage is usually arranged by a go-between and parental consent is necessary. On the marriage day, the bridegroom or a close friend goes for the bride, accompanied by as elaborate a procession as the family can afford to hire. The ceremony takes place at the bridegroom's home. The young people drink wine from cups joined together by a red cord, recalling an old legend about the man in the moon who said, "With this red cord I tie together husband and wife. Even though born in hostile households, their fate is inevitably fulfilled," which is the Chinese equivalent of the western saying, "Marriages are made in heaven." The bride joins her husband in bowing before a tablet to Heaven and earth and the ancestral tablets. By this act she transfers her filial loyalty from her own family and ancestors and accepts her position as a willing servant in her husband's home.

The old Book of Rites states: "Man and woman complement each other as do Yang and Yin. Husband and wife must respect each other as if he or she were the most honored guest. Without love, there can be no union; without respect the love will be ignoble."

The gayest and most universal festivals in China are those which are

The marriage chair carries the bride to the home of the groom where the ceremony takes place.

associated with the seasons and are based upon the old ideas of Yang and Yin and the necessity of keeping the rhythmic balance between them. The village temple is the center of the festivities as it is of all community life.

New Year is the most important Chinese celebration and lasts two weeks. All regular shops, offices, and schools are closed, but food markets, flower and gift stalls crowd streets and open spaces. Peach blossoms, symbols of long life and immortality, are among the flowers forced into bloom for decoration. Mottoes are pasted over the doors of houses, for written words have magic charm to make wishes come true, and two guardians of the portals, in military dress, are pasted on the entrances to ward off evil.

New Year's Eve is the time of family reunion, reunion with the dead as well as the living. Each gift placed on the household altar has symbolic meaning; the many-seeded pomegranate suggests a growing and united family, a peach long life, a citron happiness, a piece of ivory prosperity; without spoken words, they express thanks and hopes. Candles and incense are burned before the tablets of the ancestors. The children fold papers in special shapes and address one to each ancestor for five generations. The head of the family throws them, one by one, into the urn for burning, and comments briefly on the person addressed. The holiday feast is spread for the dead as if they were present in person, with ten bowls of food and of drink, as ten is the perfect number. The members of the family bow in turn according to their rank and wait in silence as the spirits of the ancestors enjoy the spiritual essence of the food. Then the feasting begins, even if it is only an added bowl of rice. In homes of wealth course after course is served. Gifts are exchanged, there is singing and story telling, and the boom of firecrackers is heard long into the night. The first ceremony of the first day of the year is an offering to Heaven and earth, father and mother of all.

The chief spring festival comes at the equinox. This is a critical time for the sun. A writer more than two thousand years ago advised, "Color eggs, boil, and break them," as a way to help the sun break the shell that is holding back spring life. Swinging, "the amusement which gives the sensations of being immortal," and a primitive Ferris wheel, which makes it possible to "whirl through the air like butterflies," were also believed to give magical assistance to the sun; they still are popular spring pastimes. The willow, which leafs out first of all the trees, is

Then the feasting begins.

used for decoration. This is the time to visit the family graves, put them in order, share a feast with the departed, and return home refreshed by the new life of spring, the triumph once more of light over darkness.

Just before the summer solstice, on the fifth day of the fifth month, according to Chinese reckoning, comes "The Double Fifth," a festival to help the adjustment of Yang and Yin, and to protect men's interests as Yang loses its ascendancy and the power of Yin increases. Three-cornered rice and fruit dumplings, wrapped in bamboo leaves, which represent Yang and Yin as they enfold each other with equal power, are the special food for this festival. In many parts of the country dragon-boats are a feature of the celebration. They carry disease and all evil downstream.

The harvest festival is held for several days preceding the full moon of the eighth month. This is sometimes called the birthday of the moon, "the abode of the Immortals." Elaborate altars stand in front of shops and homes, decorated with figures of the Immortals and the palaces of the moon. Lanterns hang from the many tiered roofs of pagodas. Shops sell large round "moon cakes" and special toys, usually connected with the bunny, for the Chinese see a rabbit in the moon. Legends of the moon, some of which are familiar all over Asia, are repeated again and again. The evening dinner on the last night is served out of doors. In all the rejoicing in the good gifts of Heaven and earth, there is generous sharing with the ancestors and the gods, and gifts and greetings are sent to friends.

The winter solstice is a family festival, for which every one who possibly can comes home. On the preceding evening, all gather around the kitchen table to roll the small, fat, round dumplings which are the specialty for this festival, suggesting by their roundness the oneness of the family and the hope that the circle may continue unbroken. These will be cooked for breakfast, presented to the gods and ancestors, and sent as gifts.

THE KITCHEN GOD

In all lands from time immemorial, men have worshiped fire because of its mysterious power to help and to injure. In primitive Chinese homes, the cooking was done under a central opening through which the smoke ascended to heaven and through which sun and moon looked

The dragon is the central figure in the "Double Fifth" festival. In olden times the Chinese believed that the friendly dragon drove away all evils.

down upon the family. Small wonder then that each God of the Hearth became the minister sent by Heaven to each particular family, to watch over it and to report. When better houses were built, the god moved into the kitchen. If a Chinese family changes its residence, the Kitchen God with fire from the hearth is the last to leave the old home, the first to be established in the new one.

Each year a large sheet of red paper with the portrait of the god is pasted above the stove. Surrounding him are characters and pictures which suggest the prayers for the new year. Among these is usually the bat, which has become a symbol of happiness because the Chinese words for bat and happiness sound alike. From this point of advantage, he watches all the doings of the family; he is the most intimate helper and the most severe critic. At the end of the year he returns to Heaven to make his report. On the altar table before the stove, are incense, candles, vases, wine, and various foods and sweets such as he has often seen prepared on the stove below him. The family all stand by as the father presents incense and kow tows, then touches the lips of the god with honey that he may report only sweet things. His journey to Heaven begins when the father places him in the incense urn and he rises in the flames and smoke.

> "Come, god of the kitchen,
>   Old grandfather Chang,
>   Come, here is your pudding
>   And here is your t'ang (sugar).
> "Go flit up to heaven,
>   Be gone in a trice,
>   Forget all the bad,
>   Tell only what's nice."

The children enjoy the sweets the god has left behind, but the hearth seems bare and lonely until the fourth day of the new year, when in a new portrait he is back in his place. Then the family returns to its usual routine, assured of harmonious relations with Heaven and with their fellow-men.

SHINTO—THE JAPANESE WAY

THE RELIGION OF THE PRIMITIVE JAPANESE was simple nature worship; their "kami," deities, were a volcano, a river, a flowering tree—any manifestation of power and beauty. They believed that Japan was the land of the gods, who lived in its forests and mountains, on steep cliffs and in waterfalls, who "make the trees bloom" and "weave brocade of autumn leaves," who ride in the butterfly in the evening and the firefly at night. Nature, man, and the deities all have the same creative impulse, the same urge toward life and progress; all are kami. Even the soil of the land, so lavishly endowed with beauty, is sacred. "Whatever is, is divine spirit." This is the basis of all religious thought in Japan.

Japanese religion is rooted in mythology. The people scarcely distinguished between their myths and the actual facts of their ancient history. They believed that their race is descended from the gods, that their high destiny is to fulfill the divine commission, "The whole world under one roof." They think of their emperor as the direct descendant of the Sun Goddess and serve him with a loyalty as instinctive as that of bees to their queen. For the Japanese, religion and patriotism are one; the most deeply rooted emotion is love of native land. "Every true-born citizen of the land of the gods is a descendant of the gods."

No one knows what would have happened in the cultural development of the Japanese if Chinese influence had not come to Japan and put an end to their independent progress before they had framed any moral or legal code or any religious creed. Their leaders liked the emphasis Confucius placed on loyalty and obedience toward parent, teacher, and ruler, and they adopted the ethics, social organization, and written language of China. When Buddhism was introduced, the Japanese, eager as always to try any new thing, accepted it quickly. They gave the name "Shinto," way of the gods, to the native religion to distinguish it from the way of the Buddha. The two are combined in the faith of the masses, yet the innermost feelings and instinctive behavior of most Japanese spring from Shinto.

No building is necessary to make a spot sacred in Japan. A waterfall is heaven-given power coming down to earth; a mountain is the divine spirit on earth reaching upward toward its heavenly source; a grove of lofty trees is a sanctuary of the Universal Spirit. Tree-worship is found in many early religions; in Shinto it is still alive and strong. Many small shrines nestle under the branches of trees which were old before the shrines were built. Larger shrines are in the midst of groves.

The early shrine was a simple structure like a Japanese house. Modern shrines are not very different; the Japanese believe that the simplest is the most pure because it is closest to the divine age. The buildings are of wood, the most abundant material in a land of mountains and forests. The gabled roof is covered with thatch or bark. The dignity yet lightness of the roof, the fine proportions and slight curves are the chief beauty of Shinto architecture.

There are no idols in Shinto shrines, for Shintoists think of their gods as spirits, but the symbol of the deity is in the sanctuary. It is never seen even by the priests, but is kept in a box covered with a cloth.

Shinto shrines are always open, at night as well as during the day. A worshiper comes at will for his brief ritual of cleansing, communion with the spirit-world, petition, and thanksgiving. He rings a bell over the entrance, claps his hands—an ancient form of showing respect—, throws a coin or small package of rice into a box or net inside the hall, takes off his shoes as Japanese etiquette requires, then enters to pray.

The priests in charge of the shrines conduct official ceremonies on prescribed occasions, but there are no regular daily or weekly services. Upon request they hold special prayer services for those in need, perform weddings, officiate at funerals, dedicate the sites of new buildings, and invoke blessings upon new enterprises.

Often a legend connects a village shrine with some kami, who is frequently the ancestor of the clan. The shrine is the center for festivals, for common prayer in times of drought or pestilence, and sometimes for community business.

Almost every town has a sanctuary dedicated to one or more local or national heroes. Every soldier who has fallen in defense of his country has known that his name would be inscribed among the kami worshiped at some such shrine; all former sins were wiped out by his glorious death for his emperor. At the Nation-Protecting Shrine in Tokyo, a solemn ceremony of prayer and ritual deifies all those who have fallen since the last ceremony. As the names are recorded, the spirits assemble

The approach to a Shinto shrine is marked by a "torii," a gateway of two upright pillars with two beams across the top. The shrine has an open prayer-hall and an inner sanctuary, which only the priests may enter. The wood of floor, pillars, and beams is unstained, polished to a gleaming smoothness to bring out the natural graining and soft colors.

and take their places in a cabinet, which is then carried to the inner sanctuary, where ritual gives them rank among the kami, who will ever guard the nation. Even those who have died in foreign lands are believed to return to protect their fatherland. Soldiers going into battle say to each other, "I'll meet you at the Nation-Protecting Shrine."

There are over one hundred thousand Shinto shrines in Japan which have been under government control. Every detail of the ritual has been dictated. This state system was begun about eighty years ago to further the ambitions of militarists and empire-builders. It taught the people to take without question the old myths about the divinity of their emperor and of Japan's mission to rule the world. It required everyone to participate in its worship as evidence of patriotic loyalty. It insisted that State Shinto was not a religion but the cult of nationalism. It assumed that every Japanese was a Shintoist, even though he was also a Buddhist or a Christian. The military defeat of Japan has put an end to State Shinto. Some priests believe the shrines now can serve better the truly religious needs of the people.

In addition to the state shrines, there are thirteen Shinto sects with a membership of many millions. Their members, in common with all Shintoists, believe that all things are expressions of divine spirit, they worship Shinto deities, they reverence the emperor, they are loyal to their country. But they insist that true Shinto is genuinely religious and that it cannot be held in rigid forms; its spirit is free and flexible, ready to learn from experience and from divine revelation. Most of the sects have been founded by men and women of the peasant class who believed they had direct revelations. Their ethical teachings are high and they meet deep human needs. Faith-healing is prominent in several of them. The importance of right mental and religious attitudes and the power of ritual and magical practices are recognized.

Their church buildings, not unlike the shrines in architecture, are used for regular religious services with preaching as well as prayer and ritual. Their preachers and teachers, many of whom are women, carry on missionary work in addition to serving their own congregations. They engage in many forms of social work, believing that "There is no other way of serving the gods than by spending one's self for men." The most significant tendency is the freedom from narrow nationalism. Many sects teach that the demand for loyalty to one God who loves all men as His children and for service to all humanity is as great as the demand for loyalty to emperor and native land.

Purification is the necessary preparation for Shinto worship. In the court of the shrine there is a water-trough, from which the worshiper dips water to wash his hands and rinse his mouth before approaching the prayer-hall.

A Shinto priest, reading prayers in a forest. The heavy rope, with frayed tassels, marks the place as sacred. Shinto priests are not a class apart from other men. They wear their white vestments only when worshiping, they do not shave the head or take strict vows as do Buddhist priests, they have no monasteries, they marry, and may have occupations other than the priesthood.

The grace and simplicity of the torii make it a fit symbol of the Shinto faith.

THE ART OF LIVING

In every Shinto home the center of worship is the shelf of the gods, on which stands a small shrine of spotless white wood. This contains tablets which bear the names of the family gods and the god of the community Shinto shrine. On either side are a cup for wine and a vase for sacred plants or flowers and, between them, a little saucer-shaped lamp with its wick floating in oil. Holy texts are placed on the shelf and, on special occasions, a small straw rope is hung above it. Wine, flowers, and light are offered every day except by the very poor, for whom three days a month suffice.

Perhaps more than any other people, the Japanese weave beauty into their daily lives. The weathered wood and heavy thatch of the peasant's cottage do not mar the natural beauty of the country. The residence streets of a city pass uninterestingly between high fences, but cherry trees and pines overtop them and, through open gateways, there are glimpses of charming gardens even in tiny courts. Except where western influence is strong, simplicity and restraint characterize the construction and furnishings of the modest homes, as well as the life lived within them.

In Japan as in China, Confucius is the teacher of the art of living. All right living rests upon the principle of reverence. Training in consideration for others begins early. The child is taught self-control, patience, and unfailing courtesy. He should never give way to irritation or anger; he should seek always to give pleasure to others. Long training is necessary to make the right behavior, the gracious kindliness instinctive. "The smile that never comes off" is a part of etiquette, which would give all possible pleasure and never cause unnecessary anxiety or sorrow. This strict disciplining of emotion makes it difficult for a Japanese to be spontaneous; he may often seem insincere. Sincerity is the highest virtue according to Shinto teaching, but the official doctrine has been that truth is what the government asserts to be true, the test of sincerity is conformity to decrees; a man may "follow the desires of the heart but never go beyond the rules."

The children of well-to-do families have private lessons in manners. The boys are taught jiujitsu and fencing. The girls learn music, dancing, flower-arrangement, and how to serve ceremonial tea. In all these experiences they learn not merely the technique of the particular art

The little child learns reverence toward rice, his staple food, the gift of his two chief benefactors, the Sun-Goddess and the Rice-Goddess. He must handle his chop-sticks skillfully that not a single kernel may be wasted.

but also how to relate themselves to the rhythm and harmony of nature. For this reason the gymnasium is called Do-Jo, the place for practicing the Way.

Japanese art is marked by restraint; the movements of the dance are mostly rhythmic swaying of body and arms, the classical dramas only suggest their tragic endings, paintings have empty spaces or mists over forest or mountains, that the spectator may fill them according to his imagination. Nowhere is this economy and control more striking than in flower-arrangement; seldom are more than five sprays used at once and often a single flower and a few leaves indicate appreciation of beauty as nature made it. There is no forcing of the human will upon nature's way and no careless waste.

To carry out perfectly the ritual of serving ceremonial tea is the most important social grace of the Japanese girl; it has also religious significance. The ceremony takes place in a small room used for no other purpose, often detached from the rest of the house. The room is unfurnished except for matting and cushions on which to sit and one beautiful wall panel or a spray of flowers; the mind must be serene, not cluttered. The guests bow before the beautiful object, then take their seats facing it.

The hostess brings in her utensils, one by one, slipping quietly back and forth. Each detail must be perfect, for trifles have power to reveal harmony and unity. There is no sound in the room except the singing of the boiling kettle, "like wind in pine trees." The hostess measures the finely powdered tea into a cup, dips boiling water onto it and beats it with her tea-whisk into the "froth of liquid jade." Each guest in turn takes "two and a half" sips from the cup. The spirit has grown calm, the mind concentrated, the little group is one in its enjoyment of simplicity and beauty. In this "religion of the art of life" the external and the inner meet; "Nature and God are one."

The guests often ask permission to examine the dishes which have been used, some exquisite in themselves, some having stories that are centuries old; there is no conversation on other subjects. Indifference is the unpardonable sin. The guest who cannot appreciate the spiritual hospitality must not come again; one who can goes out with the dust removed from his vision.

The serving of ceremonial tea has been a religious ritual for centuries. The guests enter by the garden gate, leaving the world outside. They stop at a fountain to rinse their hands and mouth; they look into a deep hole to cast out worldly thoughts; then they enter through a low door, bending in humility.

CHILDHOOD

Children in Japan have a happy life. They go with their parents everywhere; they share the simple pleasures, the love of all living things, the out-of-door excursions. They may romp to their hearts' content, but when they come into the house, they leave their dirty shoes and their rough manners at the door, for cleanliness and order are the first law. Training in consideration for others begins early. In school they are told the old, old tales of filial sons, which have been handed down in China since the time of Confucius.

Under the old regime the Japanese was trained to be the most unquestioning patriot in the world. Every morning school children bowed toward the imperial palace. On the birthdays of emperor and empress and other designated occasions, Shinto priests conducted services in the schools. School classes visited the local shrines to honor their ancestors and to recognize their dependence upon the kami and their own responsibility. During holidays and vacations, they were taken on excursions to historic and religious sites, all at government expense. This not only made the geography and history of their country more vivid to them but also strengthened their faith in the unique greatness of "the Land of the Gods" and their good fortune in belonging to it.

MARRIAGE

"A woman must look on her husband as if he were Heaven and must serve him with all worship and reverence." This old-time code is still accepted by most Japanese husbands and wives.

There is a popular Japanese mystery play based upon an old legend that the gods assemble on the first day of the tenth month to arrange all marriages for the coming year. In actual life go-betweens carry out these decrees of the gods.

When a Japanese girl marries, she ceases to be a member of her father's family. As she leaves her home, she is dressed in white, for white is the color of mourning. When she reaches the groom's home, at

The birth of a baby is registered at the local shrine; he is presented to the local deities. The priest waves over him the gohei, the symbol of purification seen in all Shinto shrines. This is the child's naming day and the name is carefully chosen as an omen of good luck. A popular name for a boy is Sakae, which means glory; for a girl, Kiku, chrysanthemum.

which the wedding ceremony takes place, she puts on the ceremonial kimono, black with rich designs across the bottom and the crest of her new family. The ceremony itself is a family affair, in which the bride and groom in silence sip rice wine, "saké," from three red lacquer bowls until each has been used three times. Then they offer wine to their parents. The bride removes her veil, and guests enter for the festivities. The tortoise and stork, symbolic of long life, are favorite decorations, as are little figures of an elderly man and woman, genii of two famous old pine trees, whose song of blessing is sung.

As a rule there is no religious emphasis in a Shinto marriage, but sometimes marriages are consecrated by Shinto priests at the sectarian churches and even at state shrines.

THE CREATION MYTH

Japanese children learn pride in their country as they hear the story of the beginning of their land. One day, according to the legend, there appeared, over the primaeval, turbulent ocean, Izanagi and Izanami, father and mother of all, who descended from heaven on the Floating Bridge, perhaps a rainbow, to see what was below. Izanagi stirred the rolling sea with his long sword; as he lifted it, drops of water fell and formed a tiny islet upon which they landed. They had many children, the wind and the mountains, the woods, plains, and rivers, and the eight islands which became ancient Japan. Upon the birth of fire, Izanami died of fever and descended to the lower world. So began the contrasts of life and death, light and darkness—the Yang and Yin of the Chinese.

After Izanami's death, the Heaven-illuminating Deity, the Sun-Goddess, was born from Izanagi's left eye and, from his right eye, the Guardian of the Moonlit Night and from his nostrils, the swift, impetuous Deity, the Storm-God.

Izanagi gave the Storm-God the sea as his realm, also the underworld, whence come earthquakes and volcanic eruptions. He was impetuous and unruly. Often he raged across the country, destroying the crops which his sister's bounty had produced. On one occasion Amaterasu, the Sun-Goddess, hid from her brother in a cave. The whole world became dark. In spite of the entreaties of millions of gods, she refused to come out. Finally, one goddess danced and all sang and made

Izanagi and Izanami, who, according to ancient mythology, were creators of the Japanese islands, descended from heaven on the Floating Bridge to see what was below.

99

merry. Curiosity got the better of Amaterasu; she made a little hole and peeked; immediately the other gods seized her and drew her out and stretched a rope of straw about the entrance to keep her from going back. The universe was bright once more. Peace and order were restored. The Storm-God was banished to the west coast of Japan where his descendants have reigned ever since.

Later, the Sun-Goddess sent her grandson, Ninigi, to the Eight Islands with the commission, "Go and rule. And may our imperial lineage continue unbroken and prosperous, co-eternal with Heaven and Earth." Ninigi took with him a sword, a mirror, and a jewel—the chief treasures of the imperial household to this day. His great-grandson, Jimmu Tenno, is considered the first human emperor. He founded the imperial dynasty, which has continued until the present, about two thousand six hundred years.

THE SHRINE OF THE SUN-GODDESS

The holy of holies of the Shinto faith is the shrine of the Sun-Goddess, Amaterasu, at Isé. At the end of a long avenue, shaded by towering cryptomeria trees, stands the Inner Shrine, half hidden among the trees of the park. Pilgrims take a bypath which leads to the Isuzu River, purify themselves there, and then approach the shrine. Through the protecting fence, they see the impressive, simple structure, clap their hands, and bow in worship. Only the priests and the royal family may enter the enclosure, for in the innermost sanctuary in a casket of pure white wood, wrapped in silk, is the mirror into which the goddess gazed and which still holds her reflection. This she gave to Ninigi when she sent him to establish the divine race upon the Eight Islands. At this shrine, emperors have reported important national events to the goddess; here Hirohito sent messengers with news of Japan's defeat and with prayers for forgiveness. Here every peasant, every artisan wants to come, that divine blessing may prosper his work.

Although Isé has been a sacred site since the first century, the buildings are not old. From time immemorial they have been rebuilt every twenty years, that there may be no decay or impurity. The shrine is thus a symbol of the eternal state which endures through all change. From the wood of the former temple, tiny charms are made. One who wears such a charm has upon his own person a bit of the dwelling-place of the goddess herself with all her mighty protecting power.

The worship of Amaterasu in early Japan was in part nature worship. As the sun, she was the source of all life's energy and helped in the development of agriculture. As goddess she was more; she furthered the peaceful social order which women desire and she was the peace-maker among warring clans which came under her sway. Now, at Isé, nature worship is no conscious part of the reverence paid her; she is the ancestral deity in the Land of the Rising Sun.

Amaterasu is unique among the deities worshiped in the living religions of the world in that she is the only goddess to hold the supreme place among many gods, and she alone has been believed to have a direct descendant on earth. Every emperor of Japan has claimed divine descent from her.

THE SHRINE OF THE RICE-GODDESS

One of the most popular deities in Japan is Inari, the Rice-Goddess. Rice was the chief wealth of ancient Japan and still is the staple food. So Inari is Lady Bountiful, at whose shrine even the poorest drops a coin and shouts his prayer, hoping it will be heard above all the others.

The whole country-side is dotted with little shrines guarded by stone foxes, often speckled and spotted with lichens and moss. These are Inari's messengers and the guardians of her granary. One fox holds the key securely in his mouth while another holds a scroll which tells how to be prosperous; good advice if any one had a chance to read it!

The most imposing Inari shrine is near Kyoto, Japan's ancient capital. All day crowds come and go in the courtyard. Foxes keep guard.

Children like to buy rice in small bags to scatter on the altars, and then watch the pigeons eat it up. The mother often buys a fortune, written in big black characters upon white paper; if the fortune is bad, she throws it away; if fair, she takes it home, but if it is very good, she hangs it near the altar with humble thanks. If she is in trouble, she buys a written prayer, which she leaves at the altar, or a candle, which she puts on the rack and lights, offering her own secret prayer. There is no solemn hush about Inari's shrine unless one stays on into the night, as businessmen sometimes do, hoping that in the quiet they may find some solution of their problems.

Wooden paddles, such as women use to serve rice, are among the gifts left at Inari's shrine.

SHINTO FESTIVALS

Many Japanese festivals are survivals of ancient agricultural feasts and are linked with the changing seasons. Some celebrate national events. Some are local, but not less delightful. Many belong to a past which is being forgotten; but the customs are still observed because people enjoy them, as Americans enjoy Thanksgiving and like to decorate at Christmas with mistletoe and holly without much thought for the Pilgrim Fathers or the protective power of the greens.

At every shrine, with the music of flutes and drums, the inner doors are opened; the gods are invited to attend. Silently the white-robed priests lay offerings of food and cloth and evergreen branches upon the altar. Silently the worshipers pass before it and make deep bows.

Shinto festivals are joyous occasions. The gods are loved and honored, but not feared; they are neither all-wise nor all-powerful; even Amaterasu, when she was hidden in the cave, did not know why the gods laughed until she looked to see and then was dragged out. Temple fairs, like those in China, combine business, entertainment, and religion.

The flowers have their festivals. Every one celebrates when the cherry trees bloom, enjoying his own tree even in the smallest garden, going out to walk in parks and along avenues veiled in pink mist, and watching "cherry dances" in local theatres. Cherry blossoms have power against the plague; they symbolize the new life of spring and also the transitoriness of life.

In the autumn the Japanese honor the chrysanthemum, the imperial flower. An old tale tells how the nymph of the fountain of eternal youth sends to mortals blessings of health and long life on the petals of chrysanthemums, which are carried down the winding stream that flows from the fountain. A man who has a little stream in his garden may invite his friends when his chrysanthemums are in full bloom. Among the fallen petals, he sets afloat tiny red-lacquered cups, each carrying a subject for a poem. Each guest takes a cup and writes upon the subject it brings him and communes with the fountain of youth while he drinks saké, with which his host fills his cup.

"*Hear no evil, speak no evil, see no evil.*"

—OLD WOODCARVING AT NIKKO.

In March all little girls celebrate the Dolls' Festival; sometimes families that have no little girls celebrate it too. Dolls, handed down from generation to generation, preside in state.

For the Boys' Festival a pole is set up outside every house, from which float carp-kites, as many as there are boys in the family. As the carp can swim upstream, the boy who grows strong and sturdy will overcome all difficulties.

New Year, according to Shinto reckoning, is the universal birthday of all Japanese, for, as in China, age is counted by the number of years in which a person has lived. A child born in December has two years to his credit when January comes and every one's age advances one year.

Homes are decorated for the New Year both inside and out. Before the doorway stands a pine tree or branch, to which sprays of plum and bamboo are fastened; the pine is the emblem of courage that endures through all misfortune, the bamboo of uprightness and constancy, the plum of fragrance and hope as it is the first flower of the spring. Few go to bed on the last night of the year. At dawn they go to the shrine for early morning "prayer in the four directions." Returning home, the family gathers for silent worship before the richly decorated god-shelf.

☆　　☆　　☆

Fujiyama is the most revered mountain in Japan. During many months, the great crater summit is covered with snow, "like an azure fan hung low against the golden sky," but in the summer its enormous crags, scorched rich red, golden brown, and purple by the heat of long-past eruptions, stand bare except for patches of snow in protected gullies. Then it is that thousands of white-clad pilgrims ascend the mountain. At one of the simple shrines that mark the beginning of the trails, they wash their hands in fresh water from the mountain springs, worship, and begin the ascent free from all evil.

It is well to stop overnight at a shelter near the top and then, long before daylight, continue the ascent. The mat that every pilgrim wears on his back is laid on the rude floor and marks the space to which the owner is entitled for the night's rest. The old clock ticks away the short hours, the little lanterns smoke, the pilgrims sleep. Even before the care-taker rouses the group, some of the more devout are awake, kneeling with faces toward the summit, lips moving in silent prayer, and bells tinkling faintly as heads bow to the floor.

Soon all are astir and ready for the last steep climb that will bring them to the summit. Here they pause to welcome the glory of another day and to enjoy the vision of thirteen provinces and the island-studded sea, spreading out far below. They bow their heads; then worship at the little shrine. When they have descended to the plain, they look back with even warmer affection upon Fujiyama, the "God Protector watching over Japan."

The God Protector watching over Japan.

The majestic bronze Buddha Amida has sat for seven hundred years in unbroken calm at Kamakura, not far from Yokohama. There is strength, dignity, and eternal peace in the stately figure, absorption and complete detachment in the half-closed eyes, limitless repose, gentleness, tenderness in the calm face. Here is supreme self-conquest and infinite rest.

110

THE WAY OF THE BUDDHA

BUDDHISM does not belong to any one people or country. There are Buddhists in India, Ceylon and Siam, in China and Japan, and even in England and America. They are called Buddhists because they all revere one man and try to follow his way of living. His name, Siddhartha Gautama, is now almost forgotten. He is known as the Buddha, the Enlightened One.

Buddha lived more than five hundred years before the time of Christ in northern India, within sight of the snow-covered Himalayas. His father was prince of the Sakya clan of India. Buddhists love the traditions of his early life. His mother, like other Indian women of her time, wanted to give birth to her first child in her parents' home and one spring morning she started on her journey. But before she reached her destination the baby was born while she rested in a grove. Her maidens screened her with their long saris; the branches of the trees sheltered her and dropped their blossoms; bees hummed and birds sang.

There was celebrating in both families and among their neighbors, for a warrior son was born to inherit his father's kingdom. His early training was that of the ruling warrior caste. His teachers instructed him in all the arts and skills of a knight. He was a handsome youth with a charming manner and pleasing voice. His father complained at times that he loved pleasure too much. Yet he did everything to protect him from any knowledge of the hard things of life; he never allowed any old or sickly person to come onto his estate, that his son might enjoy life undisturbed.

One day when Siddhartha went for a ride in his elegant chariot, he saw, for the first time in his life, an old man. He asked his charioteer who this might be, bent and trembling. When he was told that old age comes to every one, the young man was greatly troubled. Soon they passed a sick man and again he asked the meaning. Later they saw by the roadside a dead man. Then before they reached the palace, they

111

met a monk. Clad in a simple yellow robe, he possessed nothing but his begging bowl, yet Siddhartha was struck by his dignity of bearing and his serene face.

He returned home, but the memory of all he had seen and heard on that ride haunted him. He was distressed that every man must suffer, grow old, and die, that death itself brings no release, since it is followed by rebirth. He wondered how one could escape; could it be by following the way of the monk, by cutting all ties that bind a person to his own separate life and learning to enter the life of the Universal Soul?

He was only twenty-nine but he decided to retire from the world. He had a son to carry on the family and wealth to provide security for them. In the middle of the night he arose, quietly sent his servant to saddle his horse, opened the door of his wife's apartment and looked at her sleeping with their infant son, then resolutely turned away, mounted his steed, and was off. Before morning he had reached the boundary of his father's kingdom. Here he took off his rich robes and ornaments, gave them and the horse to his servant, and sent him home. He cut off his hair, put on the yellow garb of the monk, and with only a bowl with which to beg for food, he began his great renunciation. Mara, the Evil One, tried to turn him back, telling him that he should rule over the four great continents and many islands, but Siddhartha answered, "I do not care for empire."

He found two Brahmins from whom he learned all the Hindu wisdom, but that did not satisfy him. He tried a strict life of physical hardship. Five monks followed him. But in time he was sure that this was not the right path. His disappointed disciples left him and he went on his lonely way, still searching.

One day after six years he came to a broad-spreading tree near Gaya. He sat under it, motionless, all through the day and into the night. There he found Enlightenment; his search was over. For forty-nine days and nights, he remained in this sacred spot, having neither food nor drink, absorbed in the glory of his new insight. Mara, who had followed him unseen, now appeared to tempt him again, saying that ordinary men would never be willing to give up life as they were accustomed to live it, with all its little possessions and pleasures; he should not try to teach the great Truth; he should keep it for himself and never return to the life of the world. But Siddhartha rebuked Mara saying, "The soul cannot be shaken by thee any more than the Himalayas by the wind."

Young prince Siddhartha in meditation.
—6TH CENTURY STONE.

After this experience, Gautama was called the Buddha, the Enlightened One, and the tree was the Bo-tree, the tree of wisdom.

Gautama went to Benares where he met the five monks who had been his disciples. In a deer park near the city he preached his first sermon to these five and "set in motion the wheel of his teaching." He told them that there are three paths from which a man may choose— the path which seeks worldly pleasure, the path of self-mortification, making the body suffer just for the sake of torturing it, and the middle path. The first two are not worthy of a man, for in each case he is thinking of himself; the middle path alone leads to selflessness and peace.

He taught Four Noble Truths. The first is that to live means to suffer; some suffering cannot be avoided. The second is that suffering is caused by man's desires, many of them selfish and grasping. The third Truth follows from these; to do away with suffering, one must give up self-centered craving and insistence upon "me" and "mine." And the fourth Truth is that one can train himself to give up desires and so free himself from evil by following the Middle Path.

There are eight steps in this Middle Path.

Right views—to be open-minded; to face facts; to accept the Four Noble Truths.

Right aims—to want that which has true value and which everyone may share.

Right speech—to say only what is true and kind and not to talk too much.

Right behavior—to keep one's best self always in control; not to steal, kill, lie, be impure, or drink intoxicants.

Right way of earning your living—to work in a way which will do no harm to any person or animal.

Right effort—to prevent and uproot evil; to cause and cultivate good; to endeavor always to overcome ignorance and selfish craving.

Right mindfulness—to keep one's mind alert and watchful; to do no evil because of thoughtlessness.

Right concentration—to sit long and quietly, withdrawn from all external objects, with all thought turned inward until there comes enlightenment, as it came to the Buddha himself.

Salvation is enlightenment. Each man can attain it in this life through selflessness. This is the supreme joy. This is Nirvana, complete peace and unending bliss.

After he had found Enlightenment, love for his wife and child drew

Behind the temple at Buddh-Gaya is a Bo-tree, said to have sprung up again and again through the centuries from the root of the tree which sheltered the Buddha.

Gautama back to his home. Followed by his disciples he entered the road that led to his father's palace. His wife had waited six long years for this day. She took the little prince, Rahula, to the uppermost room in the palace and, going to an open window, she said, "There is your father, the lion of men." She dressed the child in rich garments and sent him to meet his father, saying, "Your father owns many treasures. Go and ask for your inheritance."

So he went to his father. Half timidly he followed him all day; at last he asked for his inheritance. The Buddha, looking upon his little son, thought, "If I give him wealth, he will suffer again and again. I will not give him a load of sorrow. I will give him the noble treasures which I won under the Bo-tree." Then he asked for a yellow robe and put it upon the little boy and welcomed him among his disciples. And the prince said: "Twice blest of fortune am I whom my friends call 'Lucky Rahula,' for I am both child of the Buddha and a seer of Truth."

The Master told his friends of the glorious middle way. They rejoiced in the new freedom of spirit and began the self-discipline which should make it possible for each one to work out his own deliverance.

Gautama went back to the forest to train his disciples. He did not plan to start a new religion. Like the Hebrew prophets who lived at the same time, like Jesus almost six centuries later, his purpose was to purify and deepen the religion of his people. He said, "I have seen the ancient Way, the old road that was taken by the Awakened Ones, and that is the path which I follow." He retained many of the Hindu practices and beliefs, but he did not want people to fear the gods or the priests or to worry about the fate of their souls. He approached the problems of human life as a psychologist. He said that no one could know Brahman or the gods, and so discussion of them is of no use. What a man is and is to be depends upon himself. A man's soul is not a permanent thing, but is made up of constantly shifting feelings, ideas, and acts of will. What he thinks and what he wants have the most influence on his life.

Many followers joined Gautama and with them he founded an order of brothers or monks. He laid down ten rules for them. The first five are included in the "right behavior" of the Middle Path—do not steal, kill, lie, be impure, or drink intoxicants; the others are part of the discipline of their monastic life—do not eat solid food after mid-day; do not share in worldly amusements; do not wear ornaments or elaborate clothes; do not sleep on a raised or broad couch; do not receive gifts of money.

The monks traveled and taught nine months of the year, going out singly or by twos. They were not priests, taking charge of religion for others, but teachers, making people conscious of their own responsibility. They were known by their shaven heads, their yellow robes, their begging bowls, and their gentleness. To them Brahmin and outcaste, rich and poor were all brothers, for not by birth but by deeds does one become high or low caste.

They spent the three months of summer rains together in a camp of simple huts, going out each morning to beg for food for their only meal of the day. Summer after summer the Buddha repeated his teachings, until his followers knew them by heart. So the Order of Brothers became established. Their simple confession was:

> "I take refuge in the Buddha;
> I take refuge in the Doctrine;
> I take refuge in the Order."

A women's order was founded which Gautama's wife joined; it was placed under the protection and control of the Brotherhood. Many people wanted to follow the teaching, but not all of them could leave their homes to become monks. The Master told them to keep the first five rules of the monks, to fulfil all their duties toward their families and their work, and to support the cause by filling the monks' bowls; then they could hope in their next lives to become monks and attain full deliverance. Gautama continued this work, traveling and teaching, for forty-five years.

Eighty years had passed since the little prince was born under the shade of flower-laden trees. Once more, the ancient tradition records, it was spring. An old man, weary and ill, was resting among the familiar hills of his youth, his couch spread between two trees whose blossoms fell gently upon him. He knew that he was about to die.

His anxious friends wondered how they could carry on without him. His most devoted disciple, who had been his personal servant, hid so that his tears might not be seen. The Teacher called him and said, "Do not weep, Ananda. It is in the nature of things that we must leave what is most dear to us. For a long time you have been very near to me. Be earnest and you too shall soon be free. Perhaps you may think, 'We have no master any more.' You must not think that, Ananda. The doctrine and the discipline which I have taught you are your master."

At sunrise his body was burned with ceremonies befitting a ruler of men; the ashes and bones were carefully gathered and buried in various places. Over each sacred relic, heaps of stones were piled. There his faithful friends knelt in reverence in remembrance of him.

At first Buddhists made no images of their Master, but used symbols to help them remember him. He himself had said, "He who sees the law sees me." A Bo-tree recalled his Enlightenment. A wheel became a reminder of the law; it suggests Eternal Truth, which holds for all; to turn the wheel is to set in motion the law. His footprints carved in stone recalled his tireless journeyings. An umbrella, emblem of royalty, honored him as spiritual monarch. A trident suggested the threefold "refuge" of the monk—"in the Buddha, the Doctrine, and the Order." The most beloved of all Buddhists' symbols is the lotus. Rooted in mire far below the surface of the water, it is not stained by the mud. So the human spirit may be pure, whatever its environment.

After the death of the Buddha, there was no outstanding leader, but the five hundred monks were held together by the persisting influence of his personality. They continued their missionary preaching and their gatherings during the rainy season. They repeated and discussed what their Teacher had said and done. Much later, all this was written down, divided into three sections, and called the "Tripitaka," Three Baskets. Still later the words and interpretations of other honored teachers were added. Inevitably there were differences of opinion, which became as great as those between Protestant and Catholic Christians.

Gautama had wanted to free his followers from the Hindu belief in many gods and many ceremonies as the way to secure their blessing; this, he thought, made people fear life rather than have faith. But people are not long satisfied without some god to trust and to honor. Soon his disciples began to chant his sayings as a liturgy and to pray, with him as their ideal. Many thought of him as a god and believed that they could gain merit, build up a good karma, by prayers to him.

Scholarly monks worked out a philosophy which included many of the ideas of ancient India. They called their system of faith "Mahayana," "the great vehicle," to distinguish it from the older form of Buddhist teaching which they named "Hinayana," "small vehicle."

Buddhism in India was gradually re-absorbed into Hinduism, so that there are few Buddhists in India today; Hinayana, the more traditional form of Buddhism, was carried by missionary monks to Ceylon, Burma, and Siam; it is spoken of as Southern Buddhism. Mahayana, Northern Buddhism, spread into Thibet, China, Korea, and Japan.

Ivory statue of the seventeenth century from Siam.

It is believed that the first statues of the Buddha were carved under Greek influence, which came into India with Alexander the Great. The head is round with a high forehead; the hair is arranged in short tight curls, usually with a knot on the top; sometimes a flame, rising from it, suggests the Buddha's glory. His ears are long, because of the heavy earrings which he, like other wealthy men, had worn. Often the statues are seated figures, erect, alert, relaxed—the pose of meditation. Standing images represent him as a teacher, the right arm extended from the elbow, the hand uplifted as in benediction. The reclining Buddha is symbolic of the complete repose of Nirvana and recalls the death of the beloved Teacher. This is an archaic statue in Ceylon, carved out of the native rock.

SOUTHERN BUDDHISM, HINAYANA

The faith and cult of Southern Buddhism is like that of Gautama himself. The Buddhist is taught that what he is and is to be depends upon himself, not upon any spirits or gods. What he thinks and what he wants have the most influence in his life; he must learn to control his thoughts and to limit his desires.

The monks take their teaching directly to the people. They emphasize two things, making the best use of the present and seeking peace and showing compassion, even to animals. They ask people to observe the five rules which Gautama laid down for all his followers, and teach them to recite the simple confession of faith in the Three Refuges, the Buddha, the Doctrine and the Order. The humble villager does not know the classic language nor understand the ideas expressed, but he finds joy in the music of the words and comfort in "refuges" to which he commits himself.

For the devout Buddhist the day begins and ends with meditation in the presence of the Buddha. Even when a child is too small to understand what it means, his mother may help him to kneel and touch his head to the floor, then seat him on a low stool with his little legs crossed and his hands in his lap, tell him to look quietly at the Buddha on the small family altar, and say after her, "May all living beings be happy." As he grows older he sits still as long as he can and thinks about the world as far away as he knows it, as well as about the people near him, and repeats, every night and morning, what he learned in babyhood:

> "May all beings be free from sorrow, free from sickness,
> May they be happy and free from hatred."

Each member of the family places white flowers upon the altar—

> "These flowers so full of beauty and sweet scents,
> I place in offering at the feet of the Master."

Buddhists offer sprays of white flowers with the prayer:
"May my spirit be fragrant as this flower!"
"May I never forget that, as the flower fades, so will my body die;
  may my life be more than the body!"

At night a lamp is lit with the words,

"I offer this light to the Buddha, the Light of the Three worlds.
May the light of Truth dispel the darkness of my ignorance."

A Buddhist child kneels at the feet of the parents every night and morning. To the mother the child says, "You have fed me, and cared for me; I kneel at your feet and worship you. May you live a hundred years!" To the father, "You have made me strong and trained me to be fit to come before kings; I kneel at your feet and worship you. May you live long!" And the parent blesses the child, "May the blessing of the Buddha be with you!"

SHRINES

The village shrine is open for prayer at any hour of the day. Above the altar sits the Buddha upon an open lotus blossom, himself lost in meditation. The worshiper leaves his sandals at the threshold, enters silently, kneels, touching the floor with his head, and chants softly,

"With my brow I humbly worship
The blessed dust on his holy feet."

On the moon days, the four days in the month when the moon is new, in the quarter, full, and waning, there are special services in the temple, for to the Buddhist, the moon is the symbol of life, death, and rebirth. The monks, seated on mats before the altar, chant in unison; the people, as they listen, often repeat silently the words long grown familiar. One of the monks reads from the sacred writings. The reading may last half an hour or several hours. People come and go as they please. There is no spoken prayer, no singing, no sermon, though some temples have lecture halls in which addresses are given at other times.

The first duty of a Buddhist is his own salvation. Freedom of spirit he must achieve for himself, no one can give it to him.

"Be a refuge unto yourselves;
Seek not for refuge in others.
Be islands unto yourselves."

Yet the young have need of help to find the way; to provide this is the responsibility of the monks.

124

MONASTERY LIFE

Most boys spend at least a few weeks in the monasteries for religious training. Their heads are shaved and they wear yellow robes. They share the life of the monks. After early prayer, they go to the homes of generous Buddhists, where their begging bowls are filled with rice; sometimes they chant a hymn or ring a gong to announce their presence. The morning service of the monks comes after their return. Before noon, they eat the one meal of the day. In the afternoon the boys learn the ten precepts the Master laid down, the eight steps of the Middle Path, and many beautiful sayings of the Awakened One, which are chanted in their services. They are taught the two cardinal virtues —wisdom and compassion; the two mottoes—"Strive diligently against ignorance" and "May all beings be happy." Each boy should gain spiritual independence.

> "Like a lion not trembling at noises,
> Like the wind not caught in a net,
> Like the lotus not stained by water,
> Let one wander alone as a rhinoceros."

He must not believe anything merely because it is tradition or upon the authority of a teacher, but only because he finds it reasonable and a blessing to himself.

Yet a man cannot develop himself alone. Love is as necessary to growth of the spirit as fresh air is to physical health. Only through love can one free his will from selfish passion and desires.

"Hatred does not cease by hatred; hatred ceases by love."

"When some one curses you, you must not be resentful."

"Overcome anger with love, evil with good. Conquer the mean with generosity, the liar with truth."

"Treat others as you treat yourself."

Buddhist boys, like all others, ask answers to many questions about what happens when the spirit leaves the body. They learn that a man reaps what he has sown; no good deed is lost; every evil deed brings its consequences; actions are reborn in their effect as when a fresh candle

Many figures of the Buddha, all alike, in a monastery cloister suggest his unchanging nature.

is lighted from the flame of a dying one. It is not the soul which survives death, as Hindus believe, but character.

Most important of all, the boy comes to understand something of the unique greatness of the Enlightened One, whose own person was the finest demonstration of his teaching, whose influence has spread to many millions "the far-blown fragrance of his own tranquility." The Buddha is a pattern of what each man may become, for Gautama was not born a Buddha, but made himself one. Buddhahood, Enlightenment, is possible for all.

The young novice may decide to join the Order permanently. To give up the son is a great sacrifice for the parents, but they believe that they will gain merit through him. His ordination is a strict and impressive ceremony. After a night of fasting he is dressed in princely robes; then, in the presence of the monks and his friends, he reenacts the great renunciation of the Buddha. His head is shaved, he casts off his fine garments, and puts on the yellow robe; he makes his vows as he "takes his refuge in the Three Jewels—the Buddha, the Doctrine, and the Order."

Many buildings in southern Asia have been made holy by Buddhist tradition. In Ceylon, the ancient Temple of the Tooth was built to treasure one of the teeth of Gautama. In the temple court at Anuradhapura there still grows a descendant of the sacred Bo-tree, which was planted there by a daughter of the Emperor of India in the third century B. C.

The glory of Bangkok, the capital of Siam, is its temples—more than one hundred of them. The exterior walls are of tile or sparkling glass or precious stones or mirrors, set in carved and gilded wood or plaster. The gables are sharp and the ridge-poles represent serpents whose upturned heads make long slender horns at the lower end.

At Rangoon in Burma stands the most impressive Buddhist building in the world, the Shwe Dagon or Golden Pagoda. Golden from base to summit, this radiant pagoda rises above all its surroundings. The people of Rangoon look down the streets for glimpses of it; they see it between the trees as they stroll in the parks of the city; they look to it as they offer their morning or evening prayer. The setting or rising sun makes its glowing peak a flame of fire, reaching to heaven. People come at all hours, even at night when small lights encircle and outline the pagoda, when the pavement of the terrace gleams in the light of the tropical moon, when the bells make soft music in the gentle breeze, when the Buddha's own calm rests over all.

The Temple of the Tooth, Kandy.

129

Dazzling splendor of roofs and spires in Bangkok.

Buddhists in Rangoon look toward the Golden Pagoda as they offer their morning and evening prayer.

NORTHERN BUDDHISM, MAHAYANA

Mahayana spread into Thibet, China, and Korea. It reached China about the time of Christ, brought by travelers from India. Its teachers built up an imposing system of thought. They wanted to fire the imagination and to make clear how impossible it is to measure the Infinite. They spoke in exaggerated language of millions of aeons of time and myriads of Buddhas and vast spaces with room enough for all. They made many images and taught that, whichever idol a person worships, the real object of reverence is the Buddha-nature greater than them all, for from all time the Eternal Buddha has been leading men to the light.

Every age, the Northern Buddhists believe, has had its Buddha. Gautama is the Buddha for our age; after him will come another. They think of him as a revelation of eternal and universal truth more than as a man who lived in a definite place and time. Buddhahood, Enlightenment, is possible for all. Sometime even the gods will forget their separate existences and the devils will enter Buddhahood. Evil and hell cannot last forever, for goodness and truth alone endure.

Man is not dependent upon himself alone in his efforts for self-mastery and insight. There are divine helpers along the way, especially the Bodhi-sattvas. The Bodhi-sattvas are future Buddhas, saints who are enlightened enough to pass at once into the eternal bliss of Nirvana, but who choose to be reborn again and again that they may help others. Even when they cease to be reborn, they do not enter Nirvana but remain in heaven, accessible to man's prayers.

This is one of the most distinctive ideas of Northern Buddhism. It had its inspiration in Gautama himself. Some of his disciples might be intent upon their own salvation, but others caught his spirit of compassion, seeking the welfare of all, sending out their thoughts and yearnings where their actual service could not go, believing that even their sufferings would benefit others.

Next to Gautama, the Buddha most highly honored in Northern Buddhism is Amitabha. Through many ages as a Bodhi-sattva, he acquired such great merit that whoever meditates upon him and calls upon his name will be received into the Western Paradise where he is.

Chief among the Bodhi-sattvas is Kwan-Yin, the Goddess of Mercy.

Kwan-Yin, Goddess of Mercy, known as Kwannon in Japan, holds the place in the heart of the Northern Buddhist that the Virgin Mary does in that of the Roman Catholic. She gives children to the childless and ministers to all the needy.

—12TH CENTURY STATUE OF WOOD FROM CHINA.

loveliest of all Buddhist figures. A myth tells of her life many centuries ago and states that after her death she made her home on a rocky little island in the Eastern Sea of China, where countless pilgrims have visited her temple for hundreds of years. She will never enter Paradise as long as any one needs her help.

At first few Chinese were interested in Buddhism. They were satisfied with their lives and were concerned with practical affairs and too loyal to family ties to be interested in retiring into caves or monasteries to save their souls. But Buddhism absorbed much of the old culture and destroyed little; in time the Chinese found that it enriched their lives. The spiritual world became vital to them. The ceremonies were satisfying, and the deities gave personal warmth to religion. They heard of heaven and hell through which souls pass before rebirth and discovered that they could help their parents even after death through prayers and offerings. They learned that one son who became a monk and laid up merit for others could bring far greater blessing to his family than five who stayed at home. It is not strange that within a few centuries Buddhism had become the real religion of China.

Most Chinese today grow up under the influence of three religions. Asked what his religion is, a Chinese probably will answer, "The Great Religion"; when pressed further, he will add, "The three—Confucianism, Taoism, and Buddhism," for the Chinese believe the more religion the better. Often it is difficult to know whether a certain temple is Taoist or Buddhist. There are temples which have above the altar images of Lao-tzu, Confucius, and the Buddha; with oriental courtesy, Buddha, as a foreigner, is given central place.

Gradually Chinese influence filtered into Japan, and Buddhist monks came to teach their way of life. At first there was anxiety as to how the Shinto deities would like it. The emperor consulted Amaterasu at Isé and was assured in a dream that she herself was one of the Buddhas and that she would favor the erection of a Buddhist temple.

Then the religion spread rapidly, for both Buddhism and the Japanese people are tolerant and hospitable. More than this, Buddhism brought to Japan, as it had to China centuries earlier, a deeper life and a larger world. It also brought the arts of India and China, splendid temples, impressive ceremonies, sculpture, painting, music, and the dance.

The Lohans are thought of as the Buddha's original disciples. They are very human people for they came from all classes of men. They do not have to be treated with as much respect as the Buddhas, so their statues are often grotesque and amusing.

Japan always does more than imitate what she learns from other countries; she puts her own stamp upon it. She accepted the Four Noble Truths of Gautama; she taught the brevity of life, but softened it with her love for beauty—human life is as the falling cherry blossom, or the brilliant autumn leaf, or a boat which leaves no trace of its passing upon the dancing waves. There is one Buddha nature in all men; men struggle upward by many paths, but at the summit "the self-same smiling moon doth greet all eyes." The sensitiveness of the Japanese spirit has given charm and delicacy to the temples, the ritual, the religious art; there is a light touch in even the most profound philosophy.

There is scarcely a village or town in China or Japan without its Buddhist temple. Chinese temples follow a uniform plan. In the spacious courtyard, whose trees seem ageless, is the entrance temple, guarded by the four fierce Kings of the Four Quarters—north, east, south, and west. These might give the worshiper a nightmare were it not that in their midst sits the genial "laughing Buddha" to assure him that with all their ferocity, they are friendly. Also in the courtyard stand a drum tower and a bell tower and two large stone lions on either side of the central path, and an enormous bronze burner for incense, paper money, or prayers.

In the central building, statues of three Buddhas sit or stand upon the throne; the middle one is usually Sakyamuni, the title Northern Buddhism gives to Gautama. In front of the throne is a long table for offerings. Around the sides of the room may be various saints called Lohans.

In some city temples, there is a court of hell, the Buddhist purgatory. An encircling colonnade presents a series of representations of the punishments of the other world. Each group shows a large seated figure of the ruler of one section of hell, his attendants, who are child-size, and the puny little sinner and his tormentors, who execute the sentence with fiendish delight. To see so vividly the consequences of wrongdoing makes even the most ignorant appreciate that the path of purity, truth, and compassion is a wise course to follow. In front of each group is an urn in which to burn incense, prayers, and paper money, to deliver any dear one who may be suffering these tortures or to insure one's self against the future. No attempt is made to picture heaven except by words or paintings. The Land of Pure Delight is described in terms of jewels, fountains, flowers, and singing birds.

"The laughing Buddha," whom all Chinese love, is said to have been a corpulent monk who was an incarnation of a Bodhi-sattva some nine hundred years ago. He is not to be confused with Gautama.

Often there is a spirit screen outside the entrance to a temple—an old custom which Buddhism adopted. Since evil spirits travel only in straight lines, they will not go around the ends. This one, an outstanding example of Chinese porcelain art, is in the garden of the winter palace at Peking.

Statue of the Guardian of the Gate before the inner temple of the shrine of Buddha. His grotesque and ugly face should ward off the evil spirits.

Pagodas are the most characteristic Buddhist buildings. There are thousands of them all over China and Japan. They are usually octagonal and always have an odd number of stories, ranging from three to thirteen, for odd numbers belong to Yang and suggest Heaven. There is no superstition in the Orient about number thirteen as there is in the west.

Sometimes there is a pagoda in the Chinese temple court; more often the pagoda stands alone. The earliest pagodas were built over relics of some Buddha. More modern ones have been erected as thank offerings by grateful individuals or have been constructed by a community because of the belief that "Feng-shui," wind and water, themselves spirit-forces, can be influenced by the spiritual forces of the pagoda.

In Japan it is easy to distinguish between Shinto shrines and Buddhist temples, for in the latter there are no torii, no heavy straw ropes, no gohei. Instead there is a solid wall around the enclosure, which is entered through a massive roofed gateway. The graceful, though heavy, tiled roofs of temple buildings contrast with the thatched roofs of Shinto shrines. The temple court is often a spacious park, with smaller buildings clustered about the main temple, a bell tower, many stone lanterns, a fountain, ponds full of sacred lotus and tame fish, and pigeons everywhere. There are stands that sell gifts for the temples, toys for the children, and charms to take home. There are swings and simple games and a platform for sacred dances and public speeches, and always there are people, for temple courts are playgrounds and parks.

The interior is simple and clean, the floor covered with matting, the altar behind the rail rich but not cluttered nor tawdry. Usually there is only one Buddha image, most often Amida or Kwannon—the Japanese names for Amitabha and Kwan-Yin, Goddess of Mercy. Most of the statues and other decorations are carved from wood, the work of monks, many of whom sought by self-discipline and privations and kindly ministries to make themselves true possessors of the Buddha nature, that His mercy for all suffering humanity might find expression in their work.

Those who come to the temple to worship drop their coins at the entrance, stand before the rail, rub their palms together, offer a prayer, bow, and go out.

Camel train passing a desert pagoda in North China.

Although Buddhism is first of all a religion of monks in Japan as elsewhere, more laymen come to the temples than in China, both for individual worship and to attend the morning and evening chanting of the monks; and the monks make greater efforts to reach the people. Some sects have preaching services and meetings in which the people share in the singing and chanting, and even Sunday schools. Christian hymns have been adapted for use and modern Buddhist songs have been written.

The worship of ancestors in Japan most often follows Buddhist practices, even though the family has also its Shinto "god-shelf." The mother uses the first water heated in the morning to make tea for the dead, which is poured into little cups in front of each tablet; then she brings flowers and part of the freshly boiled rice of the family breakfast. There are candles or a small lamp, and incense, which is never allowed in Shinto worship.

Buddhism brought to China and Japan clearer hope for life beyond death. An elaborate ritual assists the soul through purgatory and may even secure his entrance into heaven. Then the body is burned and the ashes buried. A tablet bearing the new name which the priest gives the deceased is placed in the family shrine. It is the custom for one of the family to take fresh flowers and incense to the grave every morning until the difficult first forty-nine days of the spirit's journey are over; sometimes mass is said each evening. After seven days a memorial service is held; priests chant: "All are transient; all who are born, must die. Being born, they are dead; being dead, they are at rest."

The monasteries of Northern Buddhism are most frequently on hillsides and mountain heights. Far above the turmoil of life, open to the cleansing winds of heaven, the resident monks live by the Buddha's law and the visiting pilgrim finds rest and quietness of spirit. The grounds are spacious and include all the buildings needed for the life of the community, which may number several hundred. Within the protecting walls are carefully tended gardens with many small shrines and seats for solitary meditation. There are fishpools and enclosures to give refuge to animals which devout pilgrims have brought from the markets to save them from death; for the Buddha's command, "Thou shalt not kill," not only keeps the most faithful from eating meat but also teaches the virtue of saving life. In China and Japan, the begging bowl of the monk is a symbol only, for monks do not go from house to house to beg, but raise their own food.

In Japan, the Buddhist family shrine is usually in an alcove or wall-cupboard, which can be closed. When the mother has made the shrine ready, the morning prayer is said; and again at evening, there is prayer when the candles and lamps are lighted.

Buddhist monks begin the day with worship. A monk goes from court to court, striking a board rhythmically, spelling out the morning invocation. The bell in the bell-tower is struck, followed by the drum in the drum-tower, and the monks enter the main hall chanting.

Manual labor is part of the discipline of monastery life. The brothers raise their own food, do all the work of the household, and care for their gardens and grounds.

Young novice, with his teacher in Japanese monastery.

Even babies learn the Buddha's teaching that every living thing loves life and should be treated with gentleness.

Each monastery offers whole-hearted and genuine hospitality, but its primary purpose is to serve as a center for meditation and study. Buddhist monks, like the Brahmins in India and the monks of the Middle Ages in Europe, have treasured ancient literature and furthered learning.

In a typical monastery, the monks spend the long day in meditation and study with brief periods for relaxation. They are trained, when they speak, not to say "I," "me," or "mine," but to use some such phrase as "your brother" or "this monk," so that they may learn not to think of their separate selfhood but the oneness of all humanity. Silence is the rule. At eight o'clock, the big drum booms its "good night" and is followed by one hundred and eight strokes on the big bell.

A boy may enter the monastery as a novice at twelve and be ordained after a few years of training. There are nunneries for women devotees. Although their vows are not irrevocable few nuns or monks return to secular life. In a world of change and sorrow, they find peace through self-effacement and compassion. They believe that their prayers release spiritual forces and hope that their way of life will be a constant reminder that the world of the spirit is the real world.

Buddhism long ago adopted the traditional religious and social customs of the countries it entered, and added festivals of its own, great and small. Some Japanese carpenters hold an annual service for the trees whose lives are sacrificed to their work, for they remember the Buddha's command, "Do not kill," and know that every living thing, however insignificant, loves life. An old priest, burning a few leaves within a small circle of rope, said that the thin line of smoke rising straight to heaven through the branches of towering cryptomerias was a thank-offering and a prayer for the spirits of the trees which lost their lives to make charcoal.

In all Buddhist lands, Wesak is the most joyous festival. It comes on the full moon day of May. It commemorates the three chief events in the life of Gautama; his birth, his Enlightenment and his passing into Nirvana. The children make paper lanterns depicting scenes from the life of the Buddha, to decorate homes and temples and shops. They gather flowers to adorn their little shrines for the baby Buddha. Streets swarm with people going to and from the temples and later enjoying the illuminations. In some homes the day is one of solemnity rather than festivity; all except little children spend the hours in meditation and observe the ten precepts which the Buddha laid down for monks;

Procession of children with sprays of white flowers in honor of the Buddha's birthday.

the next night they go out for the celebrations.

In mid-summer comes the Festival of the Dead—All Soul's Day, Old Home Week, or the Festival of Lanterns, as it is variously called. Sons who have moved away come home if possible. Whether the dead are enjoying the blissful calm of heaven or enduring the exciting tortures of hell, Buddhist tradition teaches that once a year their spirits return to their old homes.

The first morning, the ancestors' shrine is made beautiful, and abundant food is laid before their tablets. Lanterns, elaborately decorated, hang at each gateway of the home. Then the family goes out to the graves with offerings of food, flowers, water, and incense. They hang white lanterns there and give the spirits an urgent invitation to visit them. In the temples fresh decorations and offerings are waiting, and the priests chant the sutras of the dead. As twilight falls, all lanterns are lighted and sometimes large welcoming fires illumine the shadowy darkness of the streets. Unseen and unheard, the spirits come, each finding the familiar open door and his own tablet in the shrine.

Toward evening on the third day, farewells are said. If near a stream, each family will launch a tiny craft loaded with food to carry the dear ones away; an incense stick burns at the stern, a lantern lights them on the journey down to the great sea. Harbors glisten with these many lights, and the shores are thronged with people, watching, as long as they can see, the frail barks that carry the beloved spirits.

PILGRIMAGES

The Oriental has long connected religion with traveling. To go to the old home is to visit the tombs of the ancestors, a holiday outing is often to the park of some near-by temple, and vacations are spent in journeying to the more distant sanctuaries. Buddhism has trained its followers to believe in the value of the hardships and self-discipline that long pilgrimages involve. The mood of a pilgrimage is very different from that of a festival. The pilgrim is a worshiper, seeking some higher good for himself or fulfilling a vow in behalf of others. There is happiness and good fellowship but also quietness and solemnity.

One of the most majestic places of worship is Adam's Peak, which towers above the lower mountains of Ceylon; on the summit is a "footprint on the rock," a shallow depression about six feet long. Hindus call it Shiva's footprint, Buddhists reverence it as the mark of their

The Festival of the Dead. As they bid farewell to the departed spirits, each family launches a little boat, lighted with a lantern, to carry their dear ones away.

founder, while visitors with western tradition, impressed by its antiquity, named it for Father Adam. The little shrine is only a small roof resting upon pillars, open to every wind that blows. But it is holy ground. Pilgrims of many faiths toil up the rugged path, singing as they go. Most frequently they ascend by torchlight, keep vigil on the frosty summit, and greet the rising sun with shouts and prayers.

The most sacred of all the mountains of China is T'ai Shan, "the Great Mountain," the oldest place of continuous worship of which we have knowledge. According to the most ancient records, an altar was built on its summit and sacrifices offered almost three thousand years before Christ. Here the founder of each new dynasty came to seek the favor of the god to whom he owed his sway, and every emperor brought his offering once in five years. Here Confucius stood—a carved stone marks the spot—and looking off to the distant Pacific, remarked "How small the world is!" His visit, five centuries before Christ, is a half-way mark in the history of the mountain.

Because a high mountain gives rise to streams, it was believed to have power over life. Since T'ai Shan is the eastern mountain, it was associated with spring, the source of life. The people came to think of it as itself a god, who determined man's fortune and the length of his life. Even now, in the early spring, sometimes as many as ten thousand ascend and descend in a single day.

T'ai Shan rises more than five thousand feet above the plain, towering over other peaks. The path up the mountain, "The Broad Way to Heaven," is six miles long and is paved with great stone slabs. The grade is often steep and there are six thousand six hundred steps. On the face of the rocks are many inscriptions; one near the summit reads, "Approach cautiously the Region of Beauty." Wherever possible there are little terraces with growing grain. Cypresses and cedars cling to the steep mountain side, wild flowers bloom in the crannies. There are numerous shrines along the steep ascent and near the top little rock-hewn caves, where devout monks are fulfilling their vows of life-long confinement and silence. On the summit, among many pillars and inscriptions, are three temples, Confucian, Buddhist, and Taoist. Most pilgrims visit all three, burn their incense, and prostrate themselves.

Standing on this wind-swept summit, with foot-hills far below and the flat plain stretching away to distant horizons, it is easy to understand how great thoughts of God and man came to the simple men of early days.

☆　☆　☆

The Orient is changing rapidly. Even the humblest people live in a larger world. Many more are learning to read; scientific methods of agriculture are changing the lives of thousands; other thousands are leaving the country to work in city factories. Women have more freedom and influence outside the home.

All this has its effect upon religion. Yet people of every nation love their own culture and customs. In every country the religion of the future will be built upon the religion of the past.

Those who know most about religion recognize that no people, no country, no age has a monopoly of faith, truth, and goodness. The simple, deep desires of all people are the same; the fundamental religious truths are universal and therefore the more compelling. To share the will and purpose of God is to find one's best self. To link the small individual life with the larger life of humanity gives man dignity and value. In every faith, some have found that for which all search, unity between the worlds of the seen and the unseen, meaning for human life as part of the One Life, the God who is in all and above all. The world of the spirit is man's true home.

THE PHOTOGRAPHS

INDEX AND GLOSSARY

Suggestions for pronunciation:

Oriental languages stress every syllable the same without marked accent.
Many sounds cannot be accurately represented by English letters.
Vowel sounds are more like those in continental European languages than in English.
Consonant sounds are usually similar to those in English except in China, where the
    Roman letters chosen to represent the sounds are often poor selections.
B indicates Buddhism; C, China; H, Hinduism; J, Japan; S, Shinto.